Freelance Newbie

A Beginner's Guide to Finding Clients, Making Money, and Building Your Web Development Empire

RealToughCandy

"It's hard to beat a person who never gives up."

-Babe Ruth

Table of Contents

Preface..5

Introduction...7

The Business Plan vs. Winging It...11

Your Workspace...22

Setting Up Your Website...28

Your Services...32

How Much Should I Charge?..37

Starter Clients..48

Finding More Clients..55

The Name Game...67

Customer Service (Still Matters)...72

The Proposal..78

Writing That Contract...81

Developing..83

Post-Noob...93

Conclusion..97

Appendix A: Do I Need To Know WordPress?......................98

Appendix B: Common Client Objections...............................100

Preface

In 2017, I finally took the plunge. After months of internal dialogue and debate, I started a YouTube channel focusing on web development. From freeCodeCamp coding challenge walkthroughs, to JavaScript tutorials, to debating Gimp vs. Photoshop, my early videos drew a core audience of web enthusiasts from around the globe. While some subscribers stayed in the digital shadows, others were quick to share their own developer experiences in the comments section.

As I kept producing more videos and drawing a bigger audience, something interesting started happening. Whenever I did an "insider" video on freelance web development – whether it was about my marketing techniques, how much to charge, or even personal client-from-hell stories – more and more subscribers would come out of their comfort zone to ask follow-up questions about this freelancing thing.

After over a year of getting freelance questions from eager web developers, I decided to write this book. I feel compelled for two big reasons.

Firstly, there just isn't enough affordable, real-world information out there for beginning freelance web developers. Many materials focus on general pointers like "find a niche" or "focus on your dream" – is that really worth $350 or $800 to most people (or even $10)? Other freelance materials simply aren't specialized enough to address the specific needs of web developers, like designing web development services and packages. My educational materials focus actionable, real-world steps you can start implementing right away, rather than theoretical filler and fluff you've no doubt come across many times before.

Secondly, I'm a big believer in entrepreneurship – working for yourself is possibly the most rewarding decision you can ever make. And web development is just about the perfect discipline to pair with entrepreneurship, because there are a *lot* of problems out there that are desperate to be solved with your tech skills. I love sharing this with people and helping them find independence and financial freedom.

Think about it: When you pursue freelancing, no longer are you working long hours on somebody else's dream – you're now working on *your* dream. **You** call the shots, **you** choose your clients, and if you decide to go full-time with your freelancing, **you never have to clock in, clock out, or deal with bad**

bosses ever again.

Coming up, you'll read about my first experience with a web development client and I'll warn you: it's not pretty. But even though my first experiences were pretty terrible, I didn't give up. And that is the key ingredient to getting started – and succeeding – with freelancing: **do not give up**. My persistence allowed me to transform my own negative experiences into what academia calls "teachable moments" – unplanned opportunities to gain insight. With that insight, little by little I evolved my pitiful and disjointed efforts into an organized business operation that represents *me*. With persistence, planning, and motivation, you too can make a successful career out of freelance web development. Now let's get started with freelancing!

P.S. I want to give a special thanks to George M. and Paradoodliedoo! for their very valuable beta testing. I really appreciate the honest feedback. You rock!

Introduction

The first webpage I ever built was on Geocities. Remember Geocities? It was Yahoo's free web hosting site that allowed anybody with an Internet connection to build a webpage. As a teen, I was a real prankster and built a satire page for my classmates to visit when we had classes in the computer lab. I reveled in my alone time with the Geocities drag-and-drop editor.

I knew some basic HTML back then, but it wasn't until years later in 2014 when I started flirting with the idea of becoming a professional web developer.

Finally, in 2016, I took on my first freelance web development client.

But unlike my Geocities adventures, where everything was funny, light, and met with delight from my peers and disdain from my principal, this experience was a train wreck.

My client owned a highly-reputable orthodontic business and she had recently developed a proprietary product for cleaning teeth. While in-store sales were doing great, she was ready to break into ecommerce. According to her husband, the duo had gone through multiple developers and consultants, including a relative who was also a full-time car salesman three states away. For one reason or another, none of these people had been able to complete the project.

Our first meeting at my local coffee shop went fine. While the story of the car salesman gave me a mild knot in my stomach, I remained highly optimistic and excited – after all, this was my first "real" freelance client. I asked a lot of questions, took a lot of notes, and we wrapped up the meeting with smiles and handshakes. I was confident I would hear from this motivated couple soon.

Sure enough, I received a call a few days later and was absolutely ecstatic. I didn't even have a portfolio or price list yet and I was already getting a callback from clients with cash!

That's when things started going downhill.

"Hi Candy, this is Jim. Hey, Tina and I want to meet with you again. Can you come down to the office tomorrow?"

I felt that mild knot again in my stomach: their office was in another city, over an hour away, and I wasn't getting paid for this meeting. But once again, the thrill of me being pursued by a freelance client overpowered any physical manifestation of doubt I may have had. I didn't even ask them why they wanted to meet – I happily obliged, because clearly we were about to close the deal.

It was a Sunday and their office was closed, so Jim unlocked the door for me and led me to a dark room in the back. Tina was there with the lights off, squinting and mumbling at something on her computer. The two discussed work-related issues for a few minutes before acknowledging my presence. But hey, they're busy business people, and I really want them as a client. So I waited.

After a few more minutes, Tina looked up from her computer, gave Jim the nod, and then he gave me the rundown: they did actually have a website built already from their car salesman nephew, but he got stuck on something and didn't have time to complete it. Tina sighed, got up from her desk, and scurried to a huge printer outside her room while quietly chanting, "I hate her. I hate her. I hate her," as scanner lights illuminated the dim hallway.

Things were getting weird, but I figured it was just the cost of doing business.

This dysfunctional blob of a meeting continued on for over an hour. I was finally getting impatient with the misdirection, and looked for an opportunity to interject. While Jim brought up the topic of geofencing and worked himself into a near-mania with the possibilities, I looked at my notes, confirmed what their development problems were, discussed how I could solve those problems, and stated the next steps in the development process.

They seemed receptive to my ideas, especially after I explained the importance of a site that featured responsive web design (a major feature missing from the current site) and embedded videos.

"We'll get back to you soon," Jim said.

I got in my car and drove an hour back home.

Three days later, I get another call.

"Candy, it's Jim here. Say, listen. I've got one of Tina's co-workers who claims she can get this thing built for free."

I froze with disbelief, stunned with silence.

He continued, "Now, I don't know if she's telling the truth or not, but I want to get together with you for another meeting. And she wants to tag along with her husband to see what this website stuff you do is all about."

I was shaking a little at this point with anger, betrayal, and embarrassment. Deciding to deal with the emotional fallout later, I said very calmly, "Jim, we can meet, but at this point I'm going to have to start charging you.

Jim wasn't having it.

"Charging for a meeting? I think you're being unreasonable. I mean, this could be a big business opportunity for you. I've just never been in a situation where a person charges for a meeting."

"Jim, you just told me you have a lady who can do my job for free, who wants to know how I build my websites. And you want me to meet with you all for free for the third time? I'm sorry, but no. If you all want to meet for a consultation, I do charge for that."

The line was quiet for a few seconds. Then he said, "Well, then I think we might be better off finding somebody else. Could you at least get in touch with Tina and let her know if you're still interested in revamping her personal website?"

Updating Tina's personal site was was something we had briefly touched upon at our first meeting. I agreed to contact her, and hung up the phone. Where had it all gone wrong?

Once I snapped back into reality, I sent a professional email to Tina that afternoon, letting her know that we would not be doing any business together.

We never spoke again.

Learning From Failure Is The Most Important Education

How many problems (or potential problems) did you identify in this client-from-hell story? Would you believe that I experienced two more similar stories just like this one before I learned my lessons? In this book, we're going to go over how to handle clients, the importance of staying proactive and professional, and actionable steps you can take to reduce your chances of negative experiences. Most of these are common mistakes that beginners make, and perhaps you've already experienced some of them with your early freelancing efforts.

When something goes wrong early on, it's easy to let the failure stain your perception of your career for the worse. One negative experience can make people quit freelancing – unfortunately, many people *have* quit because of that. However, the most important thing you can do in this situation is to learn from it and **press on**. Your head will hurt, you'll have days where you're absolutely exhausted, but don't give up. Your dream is worth more than that.

No doubt, dealing with low-quality clients like the ones I dealt with at the start of my career is soul-sucking, but honestly, it's a part of **every** business. The important part of it is to put everything into perspective, focus on your dream, and realize that negative people aren't going to personally help you reach your goals. They *never* do. Transform negativity as professionally as possible and press on, using that energy to fuel greatness.

As a beginner's guide, this book is designed to get your started with a successful freelance career. As you develop your skills, build your clientele, and become more business savvy, many of the topics you learn about in this book will become the cornerstone of your freelance operation. Entrepreneurship is a life-long journey, and every success and failure can serve as an educational opportunity to help you grow as a businessperson. Stay hungry, stay positive, and you *will* succeed.

Jobs Are Eagerly Waiting for You

No, really: *jobs are eagerly waiting for you*. Sometimes it's easy to become discouraged in web development, especially in the freelance niche where your competition is killing it with her SEO game, has technical skills that surpass yours, charges a mere five dollars per webpage, or brags on Twitter that Angelina Jolie just contacted him for yet *another* website tweak.

Don't let others' metrics, marketing campaigns, cheap labor, or hot gossip suppress your ambitions for success. Countless people need web services **every day**, and there are people waiting for **you** to make it a reality.

Chapter 1

The Business Plan vs. Winging It

You've probably heard people say, "I don't like to label myself." Indeed, avoiding strict categorization as a human is a natural inclination for many. People are dynamic, and our preferences and interests often shift as our lives progress.

But freelancing is different. When we enter freelance web development, we enter as entrepreneurs, not as free-flowing spirits. In this business, labeling is **exactly** what we need to do, because it shapes our career trajectory. It lets us draft a clear, cohesive business plan rather than just "winging it" and seeing what happens. Winging it is what karaoke singers do when their lyrics disappear on their TV monitor. A business plan is what freelance web developers do when they're ready to succeed.

Think of a business plan as a roadmap. This roadmap describes your business, goals, strategies, and metrics for success, among other things. Coming up with a business plan doesn't have to be some fancy suit-and-tie affair with bows on each page. It can start off as a few paragraphs in Notepad if you want, or written down in a notebook. **This business plan is for *you*, and you alone.**

In this chapter, we're going to work on the first draft of a business plan.

To prepare for this, give yourself a few minutes to think about your skills and interests as a web developer. Then, answer these questions with as much detail as possible for the first draft. It's OK if you can't answer some or have super-short answers right now (by the end of the book you will have a lot more ideas).

- Why am I doing this; what is my purpose of freelancing?

- What are my goals?

- What is my CMS of expertise?

- What niche do I prefer? (i.e. small businesses; restaurants needing online ordering; local businesses with pre-existing websites needing modernization? Can be more than one or none at all [generalist].)

- How will I market myself?

- Who is my ideal client?

- How will I make money?

- How much money will I need to start; what is my budget?

- Who is my competition and what is my competitive advantage?

- What is my action plan; what steps will I take in the next month, quarter, year?

Also think about obstacles and concerns you have with starting your freelance career. Some of these questions might take you more than a few minutes to answer. In fact, some of them might even take you a day or two or more to answer. No problem. The purpose of answering these questions is to analyze your hopes, dreams, realities, and preferences as a web developer so that you're able to execute those things in real life using your business plan as the roadmap. It's definitely something you don't want to rush through. Let's go through these questions in detail.

*Note: Feel free to take as many personal notes as you need for your freelance business. Not everything I talk about here necessarily needs to end up in your business plan, but it **really** helps when you articulate as much as possible. I have about six notebooks filled with notes for my business and my actual business plan is only a few paragraphs.*

1. Your CMS of Expertise

Web developers can't know everything. Thank goodness! Things are changing constantly in this field and it would be impossible to keep track of everything, let alone learn the skills necessary to implement the newest batch of languages, libraries, frameworks, and other tools used to build and maintain the web.

Before getting too deep into your new freelancing career, choose a content management system (CMS) that will be your go-to system. (This is in addition to your "raw" tech skills/stack like front end development, fullstack, the MERN stack, and so on.) CMSes are **so** important in this business. They let you and your clients manage digital content, while supporting multiple users in a collaborative environment. Without them, managing this content would be a *nightmare* for freelancers and clients (imagine your client navigating code bases and file systems to update a blog post, or you having to manually restricting access privileges on files and folders for each user).

Put another way, CMSes put a pretty, secure, and intuitive interface over the top of the code so that you and others can work in harmony. Without learning a CMS, you not only set yourself up for obscenely longer development times, but you also risk alienating most people who need websites.

Here are some examples of some popular CMSes:

- WordPress
- Joomla
- Drupal
- Netlify (for static sites built with SSGs like Jekyll, Hugo, etc.)
- Magento

Additionally, there are many ecommerce-based platforms that also serve as CMSes – or heavily feature a CMS component in their framework – including Shopify, OpenCart, PrestaShop, WooCommerce (a robust WordPress plugin), and many others.

My CMS of choice is WordPress due to its fast development times, plugin-rich environment, my PHP knowledge for the backend, robust documentation, a very active community – and not to mention nearly one in three websites is WordPress-based, highlighting it's reliability and ability to change with the times (in other words, it's a very marketable product!). For more information on WordPress, see Appendix A.

All content management systems essentially aim to do the same basic things like host multiple users with various permissions, offer modularity and extensibility, provide easy updates, and so on, so consider your ideal clients, your interests, and the ability to get help when you need it when you assess the ideal CMS for you. You can also test out open-source CMSes on your local machine to explore their layouts and features before committing to one.

If content management systems are new to you, no worries. Learning a CMS doesn't mean you have to sacrifice any of your tech skills or tech stacks. In fact, you'll find your existing coding and web development knowledge expanding the minute you start working with the CMS code, while building new skills specific to that CMS.

2. To Niche or Not to Niche

Do you feel confident in a specific industry or are you the type to take on any industry thrown your way? This is an important question because it determines where you'll spend your time networking, communicating, and building as a freelancer. Let's explore the pros and cons of niche versus general work.

Niche work is good because you have a very specific area of expertise; there usually aren't a lot of surprises since you've pre-filtered your client base. For example: if your niche is in the restaurant industry, it means you'll spend your days networking and building relationships with restaurateurs. You'll be designing and coding menus. You'll also be working exclusively in a sector that you enjoy.

It also means you can reuse a lot of components when building sites for new clients, saving valuable dev time.

There are two significant downsides to niche work. Firstly, the opportunity costs are high: there are a **lot** of clients outside this niche that could benefit from your expertise, but won't ever have the chance since you're focused on a particular subset of clients. Secondly, depending on the niche, it can be difficult to find clients in your local area. With niches that have a limited local presence, you'll eventually be forced to market yourself to distant clients in ways that aren't usually successful with newbies or are based on a straight-up unsustainable platform.

Opposite of niche work is generalist work. A generalist approach means you won't have any shortage of work requests: You take it all, baby. You can stay and thrive in your local area and work on building fruitful relationships—arguably the most important component in everything you do as a freelancer.

The downside to generalizing is that you're dealing with a lot more varied work requests, often working in niches that aren't familiar to you. You can overcome the awkwardness by doing your homework, but there'll be times when you wish you didn't have to Google the definition of "enthalpy" for the 10th time as you're working on an HVAC client's site.

I personally take all web development, design, and multimedia work thrown my way as a generalist, as long as I'm not dealing with a client from hell. It started out of necessity (I lived in a town of 350 people and the nearest big city was three hours away), then it became something I chose to pursue because of the varied opportunities. When the work request is suited to a tech stack or CMS I'm not familiar with and don't have time to learn – for example, a project that involves Android or iOS apps – I subcontract and serve as the project manager.

3. Marketing Yourself

Simply stated, the purpose of marketing yourself is to convince people that you a) exist and b) are the ideal person to solve their set of problems.

I don't want to be repetitive in this book, so skip right ahead to Chapter 7 for a whole bunch of ideas for this.

4. Your Ideal Client

You don't have to be BFFs with a client, but everything is easier when you get along with people. More importantly, identifying and targeting your ideal client can help your networking and marketing efforts, since you can really tailor and amplify your message.

An ideal client is subjective; identifying them as a newbie is simply a matter of thinking about who you want to work with. For me, it was (and is!) somebody with significant, obvious tech needs; somebody who owns a small business; and somebody with passion. It's always easier to communicate when somebody is passionate or interested in their work rather than jaded and burnt out – the second group tends to treat a web presence like a mandatory fire drill.

Last thing: when you encounter potential clients who aren't ideal clients, it doesn't mean you have to pass on working with them. Lots of people outside your ideal client will still be approaching you, and unless you identify them as clients from hell, you should be open to potentially developing a business relationship.

5. How You Will Make Money

This might sound like an obvious question, but how are you going to make money?

In other words, how will you produce an income from providing solutions to peoples' problems? This theme is central to every web developer career in existence, because solving problems is the essence of what you do whether you work at Google or develop forums for Komodo dragon enthusiasts.

You have your tech skills and stacks down, an ideal CMS you'd like to work with, and an illustration of your ideal client freshly drawn in your mind. In order to make money with all this stuff, you need to connect everything. But how do you do that? The answer sounds ridiculously simple: get organized.

When your business is organized, you make it *easy* to start earning money. The reason why talented people **don't** make money in freelancing is because there's something blocking the transaction. They're disorganized.

If the freelancer's pitch to clients sounds like a used car salesman's pitch, money-hungry and fast...*That's blocking her income.*

If the freelancer doesn't have a logical layout to her website, which creates a high bounce rate...*That's blocking her income.*

If the freelancer doesn't bother renewing her domain name and her site's down for a month before she realizes it...*That's blocking her income.*

The list of income blockers are endless, but again, the solution to earning money is clearing up these blocks by getting organized.

Start thinking about how you can organize your:

- communication
- services
- workflow
- website
- pricing tiers
- business priorities
- physical work and living areas

And any other area that you think could benefit from organization.

Earning money in this industry comes from developing a collection of simultaneous, interwoven processes – value is not created from a single event. When you're articulating these processes, recognize the roles each of them play. Define their relationships.

Anybody can make a website, but can just anybody organize a highly-technical array of processes? No, and *that's* where your money is.

6. Budget

How much money do you have to invest in your new business? If you were hoping the price tag would be "free ninety-nine," not dropping a penny on your freelancing career is possible...But it *is* difficult. Web hosting and a domain name for your own freelance site, transportation to meet with clients and attend networking events, and printing business cards are just a few of the absolutes you need to set up as a freelancer.

Sure, you can host your site for free with some platforms, you could walk or bike to all the meetings across town, and you can print promotional materials at home. But there's a **huge** opportunity cost with that. Your domain name with Wix in the URL looks tacky. Flimsy business cards don't make an impact. Walking or biking to distant meetings an hour away eats up a lot of time. So while you could get started with zero investment, I don't recommend that. Much better is to save up at least a few hundred dollars for your first round of investment items.

Here's the thing, though. This can only work out if you're still earning a paycheck from your **other** work. In other words, you can't quit your full-time job, have $300 in the bank and do freelancing successfully – it'll take a few months for the money to start coming in. Also, even though the business cards and gas money may only be a few bucks, your monthly regular living expenses from a mortgage to groceries still exist.

Be very cautious, honest, and analytical when crunching the numbers.

Consider doing freelancing part time with one or two clients while holding down a "regular" job until you can afford to transition to full-time freelancing.

7. Competition & Competitive Advantage

When I first discovered the word *schadenfreude*, I was filled with delight. Finally, a word for when I logged on to local freelance web developers' websites and saw their badly-designed pages! What is s*chadenfreude?* It's a German word that means you take pleasure in another person's misfortune. As an observant newbie, I was *definitely* soaking up others' misfortunes.

Whenever I noticed something they did wrong but I did right, my *schadenfreude* meter started going off the charts. Not only was my competition stumbling, but I started feeling more and more validated as a professional freelancer despite my newbie status. Some of these freelancers had been in the game five or ten years, yet right away I saw that their pages were missing major things like responsive web design, a convenient contact form, a convincing portfolio, or included things like unflattering color schemes and fonts.

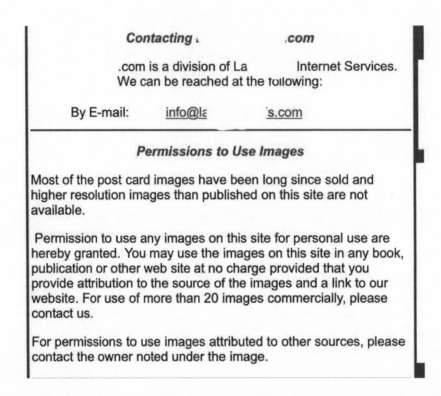

An example of freelance schadenfreude: this company has been around for a while, but stuck in the '90s with its table-based design and outdated contact method.

Aside from personal self-esteem purposes, researching your competition can give you a lot of guidance. Start by Google'ing freelance web designers and developers in your local area, along with smaller creative agencies. Take notes of **everything:** who made the top search result, what they charge, their services, their portfolio, their reviews, their niche, their target client...*everything.* You might even make a simple spreadsheet to keep them organized. If you live in a small town or rural area, search the town or city closest to you where there's a developer presence.

All of this information can be used to give you a competitive advantage as a freelancer. For example, when you're writing up promotional blurbs for your business, you can drop some unflattering (yet true!) facts about your competition – "While most outfits around the city charge anywhere from $80 to $400 for every little piece of advice, DebbieDoolittle.com offers a free, one-hour consultation along with a free business blueprint to show you how we can help you earn more revenue, gain – and keep – more clients, and propel your business to the next level."

Keep tabs on your competition, even after the business plan phase. I like to check in with my own competition every few weeks, and I also sign up for their email newsletters and other promotional blasts.

First Draft: The Business Plan

Corporate business plans are highly academic and drafted by teams of people. Mercifully, your freelance business doesn't have to report to a board of directors or deal with the bureaucracy, so you'll be working with a very scaled down version. Nevertheless, this is the key document that guides your business, so you'll want to keep it in a safe spot like in the cloud, duplicated on an SD card, or whatever works best for you.

The following example is a **first-draft** business plan to guide my theoretical freelance business.

Purpose: I'm starting freelancing because I'm ready to call my own shots. I will start off part time/weekends and go full time if I can net $35,000/year.

What I do: The CandyLand Agency offers beautiful and completely customizable web services to small-business candy and snack stores in North America. With a focus on results-driven services, my agency's core offerings hinge on WordPress with WooCommerce integration. As somebody who has a background and extensive prior sales experience in the food industry, I understand the unique needs of business owners in this highly competitive market. My competitive advantages include a free SEO audit for all customers, a two-week turnaround time, and a focus on customer service with clear communication.

How I will make money: Primary income through WordPress with WooCommerce integration. Add-on services will include copywriting, SEO, photography and video (stock), hosting, domain registration, one-on-one tutorial or consultation. Monthly maintenance packages will eventually be a significant source of income. Hosting via Namecheap and Cloudways.

Budget: $3000 to start over the next 12 months. Needs: web hosting, external hard drives, work drinks/snacks, Every Door Direct Mail (EDDM) via USPS.

Promotion: Trust-building campaign via in-person outreach to local businesses; register on Google My Business to get on Google Maps; outreach to friends and family, EDDM; blog on my company website to boost SEO, reach out to my established contacts to get featured in restaurant & service industry blogs (Steph will be really helpful for this!).

Goals:

-Secure at least one client per month
-Make $3000/month after 12 months.
-Gradually make maintenance packages (passive income) 40% of income after 36 months.
-After 36 months: $70K annual net income

Action Plan:

Now – Start process of registering for Google My Business
Now – Announce on social media & IRL that I'm doing **professional** freelancing (official announcement w/ call to action)
September 1 – freelance site deployed.
September 10 – meet and greet local restaurant managers/owners. Petey can help me out with arranging meetings with the 10th Ave. businesses.

Iterate, Iterate, Iterate

This is a good start, but finalizing your own business plan will take a few iterations as you get more ideas. As a beginner, there are a lot of unknowns – for example, it's difficult to project how much money you'll make your first year.

Web designer Brent Galloway has a nice example of a simple-but-effective freelance business plan: http://cl.ly/Q6jd

Regina from ByRegina.com has open-sourced a very clean, comprehensive business plan template available here:
https://docs.google.com/document/d/17C3YQbiyK7-i3bP26o9wxKo_J6ZKxDj9izKWXcAGJ98/edit

Either way, we now have enough information to move forward. Remember, creating a business plan isn't just a school assignment to crank out and file away once its graded. Refer to this document often, especially when you need motivation, had a bad day, or lose focus.

Chapter Summary

Whether you're highly-organized or play it by ear, a business plan is mandatory for all freelance newbies who desire sustained success. Do you absolutely need one to make money as a freelancer? No. But, if you want to start making *consistent* money, *progressively more* money, and *leveling up* to choice projects and clients while growing your business, you *absolutely need to set the foundations of your business with a business plan.*

I know it sounds academic and perhaps even boring, but trust me, a business plan doesn't have to be dozens of pages or use lots of Latin. This business plan is for you, **and you only.**

It's a blueprint that defines how you're going to succeed in the freelance game.

It's a document that keeps you focused on your goals.

It's a constant and serious reminder of why you're doing this whole thing.

Please don't skip it.

In the next chapter, we'll start setting up the physical space of your freelance business so you have the maximum freedom and flexibility throughout your workday.

Chapter 2

Your Workspace

One of the biggest benefits of freelance web development is that you can work from anywhere that has an Internet connection. Ever dream of traveling the world while earning money to fund your next destination? Does the whir of the espresso machine and strums of acoustic guitars draw you to your favorite coffee shop? Or maybe you enjoy the solitude and familiarity of your own home. In this chapter, we're going to go over your options for setting up shop.

1. The Comfort of Home

Pros:

- Tax write-off
- Money savings
- Familiar environment

Cons:

- Home/work clash
- Easy to become bored or antsy ("cabin fever")
- Still need to meet with clients outside the home

Working from home has significant benefits.

Firstly, it's a tax write-off (at least in America – check your tax laws or consult a tax professional in your country to see if you qualify). The home office deduction is available for both homeowners and renters, and the area (room, group of rooms, partition) must be used *exclusively* for your freelance business. Research "home office deduction IRS" and you will be rewarded with all the rules and benefits of this deduction.

Next, you save a **lot** of money. Most likely, you already had an Internet connection before you decided to start freelancing. You also are already paying utilities and either pay monthly rent or a mortgage – there's no extra cost incurred in those areas for setting up shop at home. You'll also save on transportation since you aren't actually going anywhere to work.

Thirdly, your home is your castle. Everything is familiar, from the color of your walls to the hue of your kitchen lights. You can wear pajama pants to work, and only your cat will judge you. When you look up, you see photos of family and friends, not strangers arguing in a parking lot. Familiarity leads to focus, which lets you get more things done during your workday.

Just chillin' and making that money from home with style.

Working from home can also be a disappointment for some, though.

While it may seem like a perfect opportunity to spend time with your family while getting paid to build websites – combining family development with web development often doesn't work as planned. Can it work? Absolutely. But development work requires long stretches of concentration, especially when it comes to coding, and family needs come first. When you're deep in code and are called away multiple times throughout the day, it can take a good five or ten minutes each time to get back into the groove. In addition, client calls with younger children present can lead to some very unexpected, unpleasant or unprofessional results.

Additionally, working from home can lead to "cabin fever" - becoming bored and restless with your surroundings. This can cause you to lose focus on your work. The key to breaking out of cabin fever if you work from home is to take breaks every hour or two – go for short walks, grab the mail, feed the birds – break your body and your mind away from the routine at regular intervals.

Finally, you will still need to find a spot to meet with clients. Meeting with clients at your home, even if you have a dedicated office, is a bad idea. By inviting them to your home for a meeting, you expose numerous details about your personal life. This is not only distracting, but also a safety risk. Clients don't need to know where you live, and they definitely don't need to know about your personal possessions, marital status, and so on.

Working from home has incredible benefits, and can be one of the biggest highlights of freelancing. However, it's not for everybody, and it can lead to work/home clashes, along with boredom and a lack of focus. If you find yourself detaching from the idea of working from home, a more socialized environment may be more appealing.

2. Shared Workspaces

Pros:

- Simulates the business environment without the price tag
- Networking potential
- Learning opportunities for growing your business

Cons:

- Distracting
- Lack of privacy
- Rules and work culture isn't yours

Shared workspaces became popular once the "gig economy" started taking off. These spaces are designed for freelancers, entrepreneurs, and other business-minded types who want the advantages of a formal office without its constrictions. With a shared workspace, rather than renting out an entire office, you pay a fee to rent out a space within a space that suits your needs. From a corner office to a seat at a table, the price you pay also usually includes access to conference rooms, open-air meeting areas, restroom facilities, a communal kitchen, and so on. This way, you can make calls, code, brainstorm, and meet with clients in a professional, clean environment.

Shared workspace configurations vary from a "hot desk" (a shared desk) to private, partitioned office space.

Since other people like you are also working at the shared space, it's an excellent opportunity to network. There may even be some web developers at your shared space – while your first instinct may be to type 'rm -rf /' in her open Terminal when she gets up to grab a beverage, this person could end up being an ally rather than an enemy. Don't be eager to spill your trade secrets, of course, but don't dismiss possibilities of collaboration or other strategic partnerships, either.

The downside of shared workspaces is that they can be *very* distracting, especially the ones that are pet-friendly. Everybody there is doing their own thing, and the minute somebody sits down to start working, another person is getting up to walk their dog. Additionally, it can be hard to get privacy with phone calls and other personal business with shared spaces unless you opt for a walled office, which can get expensive. You also have to abide by the space's rules and hours, which can mean anything from no yoga pants to a 9 PM close time.

A lot of shared spaces offer a free day pass, a sort of extended tour to get you familiar with their space. Do your research on the spaces in your local area and try and gather information from those already renting the shared space when you visit (the break rooms and kitchens are good for informal chats). What do they love about it, what areas could be improved? Take this insider information into consideration when assessing the suitability of the space for your lifestyle and business goals.

3. Anywhere with an Internet connection

Pros:

- Freedom to work nearly anywhere in the world
- Inexpensive
- Possible strategic advantage

Cons:

- Environment often not suitable for client calls or meetings
- Feels like you're always on the move – no permanency

Perhaps you've seen those videos on YouTube filmed in exotic locations by those who call themselves "digital nomads" - people who make their money via the web to fund their cosmopolitan adventures. While they usually don't do a good job of really showing you what it's like being a freelance entrepreneur (there's much more to a typical day than delicious food stands and beach blanket bingo), they do a good job at summing up the freedom you can have as a digital nomad.

The digital nomad lifestyle can be exciting, but it's not for everyone.

Feel like traveling to a new state or country for a month or two, or want to visit relatives for a bit? Get your in-person client meetings taken care of, and that reality is yours. Or maybe you just want to check out a new scene at a different coffee shop this week. No problem.

Using an Internet connection as your only geographical limitation can also have advantages in other parts of your life. Maybe you're a college student and need to be near a research library for your thesis. There's no better place to do some client work in near-silence, take a break, and then transition to your school research. Think about other things going on in your life, and see if you can find a common ground where an Internet connection would merge those otherwise-disparate engagements.

Just like with your home office, though, a library or beach towel isn't a great spot to meet with clients. If you do go digital nomad mode, stake out a few good spots where you can meet clients with minimal distractions.

Deciding on your work spot(s) can be challenging – if you're having a particularly difficult time deciding what to choose, re-visit your business plan. And you can also choose a combination of the three options, too – opting for a few days at the home office, renting a shared space one day a week, and spending Friday at a fun new location outside of your city might suit your preferences.

Remember, this is your career and you call the shots, so make choices that benefit **you** and your business. There's no supervisor telling you what you can and can't do!

Chapter Summary

It might seem silly to fuss over work locations as a newbie, but it's one of the most important decisions you'll make when establishing your freelance business. Every workspace has its pros and cons, and you'll need to sit down and assess what works for your life situation. Don't rush the decision, and re-visit your business plan for guidance if you're having a hard time with your analysis.

Now that you have a better understanding of your options for physical work locations, let's discuss your options for your digital location: setting up your website.

Chapter 3

Setting Up Your Website

You've established your physical workplace, and now you're ready to build your freelance website. This site will serve a few purposes:

- It establishes an online presence, increasing your trust factor.
- It serves as a lead generation page.
- It shows potential clients what you offer, what you're capable of, and illustrates your competitive advantage along with your understanding of the industry.
- Testimonials, positive reviews, and other social proof on the site further increases trust in your brand.

Your freelance website is your deluxe digital business card; it should highlight your abilities and trust factor.

You can incorporate all of these strategic objectives into the design and copywriting of your individual webpages. Some pages you'll want to include:

- **A home page.** This page will ideally also serve as a landing page designed to capture leads. (Capturing a potential client's email can be done in many ways, whether through sending them a free ebook/pamphlet you wrote, promising digital swag or coupons in exchange for the email address, a newsletter...get creative and think about what your ideal client wants so they'll sign up.)

- **An about page.** This page is designed to build trust with your audience – share some biographical information here related to your freelance business, your core values, mission, etc.

- **A testimonials page.** Visitors want to know you can do the job. Other people vouching for you is priceless as a newbie.

- **A services page.** Nicely-designed HTML tables work great for services, especially when you offer package deals.

- **A contact page.** An email form, phone number, and hyperlinked email address (with your domain, not Gmail or other third-party email providers). If you have a co-working space, you can list that address and post your office business hours "by appointment."

- **A portfolio page.** This page highlights your previous work. As a beginner, though, this space might be minimal. For now, you can use personal projects as placeholders (we'll cover getting "starter clients" later on). No matter who your client is, *always add context to each project you feature*. In other words, don't just embed screenshots of projects and link to the live site: tell your reader **why** these projects matter. You can use the case study format, or use PAR statements. PAR stands for Problem, Action, Result, It breaks down like this:

  Problem – What problem needed to be solved?
  Solution – What actions did you take to solve this problem?
  Result – What was the outcome of your project? In other words, what happened as a result of your actions?

  If you want to see a PAR statement in action with a portfolio piece, I PAR'd most of my first web developer portfolio. Here's an example:
  https://realtoughcandy.github.io/Portfolio/Git-Er-Dun

- **Blog.** You have a lot going on, and writing SEO-friendly blog posts on top of everything else probably isn't on your priority list at the moment. However, a blog section on your site is an excellent way to boost your SEO rankings in both local and global contexts. If you're using WordPress, Yoast SEO is a potent tool that should be in every WP developer's plugin arsenal. If you need some ideas for topics and format, check these blog sections out (note how their topics are valuable for potential customers rather than an onslaught of promotional pieces – think about how you can similarly add value while weaving in your business priorities):

https://www.scoro.com/blog/
https://www.razorsocial.com/blog/
https://www.ideo.com/blog

50 blog headline ideas:

https://speckyboy.com/blog-posts-your-web-design-clients-wish-you-would-write/

If you're looking for a strong communicator to take the long view on a project, this is your man.

A testimonial page with endorsements like this is invaluable in establishing trust with your potential clients.

Technical Components

Your portfolio's tech stack should try to reflect what you offer clients. For example, if you're a WordPress developer, use that CMS for your site. If you're a frontend developer with an eye for design, rock those CSS skills and develop something that complements your style with tasteful, unique design components. If you're building something from scratch, ensure it's responsive and have a few family members or friends test the entire site using their desktops, laptops, and mobile devices. Every glitch on your site that potential clients encounter reduces your trust factor as a new freelancer, so test, test, test.

Borrow good ideas freely and test, test, test.

During your site build (and even after), if you see a cool idea that some other agencies are using, borrow ideas where it makes sense and morph them to represent your brand. Don't go stealing the source code for Apple's homepage, of course, but do notice design trends and find inspiration in the layout, content, features, and UX/UI of successful sites, especially successful creative agencies.

Chapter Summary

Having a website for your freelance business is a must. You'll want to include pages that give context to your business, explain your services, let users contact you, and show off your best work to build trust. No matter what platform you use, always test the site using multiple browsers, operating systems, and users.

Now that you've got a good idea on how to start architecting your own freelance website, we're going to focus on a key ingredient – your services.

Chapter 4

Your Services

As a freelance web developer, you have full control over what services you offer. Further, you have the ability to bundle these services into package deals. Packages are a win-win situation for you and your clients, because they save clients' time and they make you more money. Take a look at A Nerd's World pricing page for their ecommerce services:
https://anerdsworld.com/e-commerce-web-development
You'll notice that they have four pricing tiers: bronze, silver, gold, and platinum.

The bronze level, their lowest tier, starts at $2000 and includes all the basics one would expect for an ecommerce site (cart functionality, contact form, responsive, etc.). But the package also includes add-ons like photo sourcing, a one-hour in-person brainstorm, and two rounds of revisions. Conversely, the top-tier package (platinum) starts at $30,000 and tacks on additional components like custom icons, speed tests, 50 product photos, and more.

We'll go over pricing soon, but the important part here is to solidify your services, thinking about how you can incorporate value-added services that complement your client's basic needs in a website. Here's a "fast and dirty" mockup I made to illustrate a simple way of organizing your services into tiers using HTML & Bootstrap 4:

Outsourcing Services (Or Whatever Else)

During your brainstorming sessions, you may come up with some ideas that start with, "Wouldn't if be cool if..." followed by a sting of disappointment. You would love to offer photo services and custom logos, but you don't have a nice camera and Photoshop and Illustrator aren't your thing. You scratch the idea off your services list, dreaming of one day soon where you can snag a professional Nikon and pick up some graphic design skills.

But wait. What if I told you that you **could** offer those services, along with whatever else you dream up that complements your business plan? It's not only possible, but also *profitable*, with outsourcing.

Outsourcing means you pay other people to do parts of your job. It's a double-edged sword. On one hand, cheap labor on places like Upwork and Fiverr undermines quality developer work and reduces developers to a transactional middleman (in these marketplaces, many clients simply use developers to access the cheapest price possible). On the other hand, entrepreneurial-minded freelancers can expand the services they offer by outsourcing in areas they aren't skilled in. Nobody says you have to source your talent from these sites, of course – you could employ a family member, friend, or somebody else in your network. The challenge is finding a trustworthy, quality service provider and paying them while you still make money from the transaction. It's a delicate balance, but with some creativity and planning, you can make it work nicely while sticking to your values.

Here's an example of a time I outsourced:

Sales calls are honestly the bane of my freelance existence. I really don't like them...*At all*. They're awkward, and sometimes you have to be pushy – but I'm not naturally pushy. When somebody says "I'm not interested," my initial response is usually "Oh, OK. Thanks anyway," and hang up the phone. Not a good sales tactic.

But I had recently developed a fullstack application catering to cemeteries, and knew it had some serious potential. I spent a few solid days researching cemeteries across America and came up with about 40 leads.

Instead of practicing in front of the mirror for weeks and otherwise attempt to become somebody I'm not, I decided to outsource a sales associate.

The next thing I did was think about my ideal salesperson. It needed to be somebody trustworthy who believed in my product, so zero-trust-factor freelance sites were out of the question. They didn't need to have a lot of sales experience, but they *did* need to have good communication skills. I thought about my network: who could I approach who needed employment?

Since I'm very active in the self-taught dev community, I knew quite a few people who would fit the role nicely. I also was very open about my needs in my Discord server (a chatroom based on my YouTube channel where coders come hang out). I wrote, "Hello all. I need a sales associate for a new product I developed. PM me for more info."

She looks like an approachable "people person." Would you like to be my sales rep?

Thus began my outsourcing campaign. I was ecstatic that there were actually people out there eager to perform tasks I considered absolutely grueling. The point of this whole recruitment story is that you don't have to be a lone ranger in this game – *if it makes sense to outsource, do it.* Further, you don't have to have a YouTube channel (or other social media following) to recruit tech helpers: consult your own networks, and don't be afraid to ask around. If somebody in your network isn't a designer, salesperson, writer, or whoever else, they often know somebody who is.

Lather, Rinse, Repeat

With my cemetery app, I was able to offer a unique, relevant solution. Importantly, for each sale of the basic app, I wasn't reinventing the wheel. I had a template – a sort of master document – and the cemeteries received copies of it. With a few simple edits, the app was easily customized. And because I had planned out use cases, spent time architecting the app, and talked with people who worked in admin at a local cemetery, I was able to refine my app to appeal to a massive chunk of those in that industry. This meant quick turnaround times, easy edits, and happy clients.

It also meant an efficient way to make good money. In this business, like many others, easily-repeatable transactions are a fast, legitimate way to keep the money flowing in. Don't feel like you need to reinvent the wheel for each client's basic needs! Try thinking about master templates, designs, or features that fit a lot of use cases while giving yourself room for easy customization. It's a *big* money maker.

Monthly Income Opportunities

When I first started freelancing, my focus was on finding clients who needed a website. Fair enough, right? But there was a big flaw in my thinking. I treated my business like it was a "one and done" operation where I built a website, the client paid me, and I sent them on their merry way.

It wasn't until I landed my enterprise job where I discovered the power of long-term clients. I noticed that client acquisition came second to appeasing my company's current client roster. But why? Why were companies that had already paid us still getting the royal treatment? Because they were **still** paying us. They paid us a monthly service fee that included hosting, maintenance, and they also received priority when they had a feature request (which costs extra, of course). In this way, the company was making passive income simply by hosting the site and ensuring it was safe with the appropriate security updates, all while opening the door for billable feature requests.

Consider adding maintenance packages for your clients. The big selling point with these packages is that they don't have to worry about fixing a crashed server in the middle of the night, or even navigating to the appropriate button when comes time for a WordPress plugin update. For a monthly fee, all of that can be managed for them, freeing up their time to do much more important things (like make money for their company). Think about how you can implement these kinds of features to beef up your monthly income. Freelancing is inherently unpredictable from month to month, but this can help bridge the gap between $500 months and $10,000 months.

Chapter Summary

You now have some new ideas for assembling your services and package deals. Planning, outsourcing, and creating master code bases go a long way in building your brand and appealing to quality clients. Further, monthly income opportunities can really help even out your income in the unpredictable world of freelancing. In the next chapter, we'll go over some ideas on how to appropriately price these services.

Chapter 5

How Much Should I Charge?

Attend any entrepreneurship-for-newbies webinar, watch popular freelance YouTube videos, read the slew of blog posts out there, and one of the topics that gets mentioned the most – if not *the* most – is how much to charge for your services. There's a lot of conflicting information out there, because a price can be influenced by numerous variables, including your:

- Cost of living
- Geographical Area
- Skill level
- Confidence level
- Ability to deliver quality products on time, even when things go wrong
- Desire for money
- Competitors
- Overhead
- Previous work's perceived and actual value

There's also that sneaky little economic principle of supply and demand. So, you can see how one expert might tell you to charge rock-bottom prices to earn quick clients, while another expert might tell you to charge no less than $7500 per basic WordPress site with WooCommerce integration. That's kind of a big difference!

I can't tell you an exact amount to charge for your services as a newbie. Nobody can. What I *can* share with you are some ideas that will encourage you to analyze your business in order to create a pricing structure that financially benefits you while being fair to the customer.

Remember: your skills are rare, even as a newbie.

When you create a website, develop a web app, modernize a code base, or do any other web-related work, those are tasks that are *highly specialized*. You can't just take a person off the street and say, "Hey man, code me an ecommerce site with a Node backend" or walk into a grocery store and yell, "I need a Vue developer, please!" and expect a group of eager developers to emerge from the aisles to save the day.

Capable web developers are rare, even the newer ones. They're in high demand, and demand is bigger than supply right now. This is *awesome* news for you as a freelancer.

Behind our coding activities is a science that drives a multi-trillion dollar industry. That's right: **multi-trillion**. Now, you may think hacking away at some PHP is no big deal, but when that turns into an online shopping cart that's the cornerstone of a company's business, it's a *very big deal.*

When you design and code a landing page that effectively sends a message to visitors, that's a *very big deal*.

When you are singlehandedly responsible for crafting the digital infrastructure that will serve a company, group, or individual for decades to come, that's also a **very big deal**.

Going back to my first enterprise coding job, I worked with my senior developer to create a mockup site to go along with a project proposal for a client. The proposal had a base price of $100,000.

Want to know the interesting part? We could have proposed double or even triple that and still had a chance to be awarded the contract, because we were adding *massive* value to a multimillion dollar company. And that's the first question to ask yourself when you think about your pricing structure: **What value are you adding for your clients?** When you're answering this question, be specific. Go back to your business plan. Tweak it if necessary, but you *must* understand and be able to articulate the value you are adding in order to charge appropriately for your services.

In the case of my enterprise job, the task was to rebuild an ecommerce website that sold agricultural sprayer parts. Believe it or not, that site did millions of dollars in business per year. The problem was that the site was slow and the UX/UI was in dire need of a facelift, especially since the company's competitor sites were running fast and looking fresh.

Here are just a few ways my senior developer and I would add value (which were detailed in the proposal even further with metrics where appropriate):

- We would be adding significant and direct financial value through increased sales volume, due to a faster, cleaner site that encouraged higher conversion rates.
- We would be strengthening the company's image and helping them outshine competition through a revamped user experience and user interface.

- We would increase consumer confidence in the company's online presence, paving the way for referrals, social media shares, and returning buyers.
- We would boost the company's SEO score, since Google values page speed.
- Our new buyer loyalty sign-up page would increase sales and encourage repeat transactions.

The list goes on. We translated our technical abilities into positive, measurable effects that were appealing to stakeholders, all in a digestible bullet-point format with minimal technical jargon.

Generate Value by Explaining Your Process

Sometimes, clients won't understand the value you're offering and producing, even after you've explained the features and benefits of your services. One thing that can help illustrate your skillset (and subsequent value) is by explaining your process. For example, you could publish a step-by-step guide to your web development process on your website. Here's an example:

Tony Baloneys **is a full-service digital agency.** Our flagship offering is web design and development, and we handle everything from visual design to backend development for ecommerce and other interactive sites.

We approach your digital needs from a comprehensive point of view. Tony Baloneys uses a five-phase process to ensure your brand is being effectively developed online. This process entails site Discovery, Architecture, Design, Development, and Launch.

1. Discovery phase.

In this phase, we lay out goals, performance, and recommendations. If you already have a site, our team audits it for SEO (search engine optimization), responsiveness (making sure it looks good on all devices), and usability. We create a final document with recommendations which serves as Tony Baloneys' roadmap for your website.

2. Architecture phase.

This is where we inspect the visual and technical aspects of your site to determine the optimal functionality for your end users.

3. Design phase.

Time to put things together, using industry-standard tools of the trade. For this phase, we use the guidance of our Discover Phase document we created for your site. Blueprints, mockups, and prototypes are drawn up, fleshing out the very beginning of your new site.

4. Development phase.

Your site is looking good, but now it's time to implement the functionality. Code, test, repeat. All our sites are designed and developed with a mobile-first approach, so that your site looks great on every device, regardless of screen size.

5. Launch.

We take care of all the backend work, including site hosting, addressing technical problems, and ensuring the major search engines are aware your site exists.
It doesn't stop there, though.

At Tony Baloneys, we offer ongoing support with our website and design packages, so that you're not left on your own.

Tony Baloneys is passionate about creating effective, attractive, and high-performing websites on the most appropriate platform for your project. Contact Tony Baloneys and we can discuss your needs as a small business that's ready to make an impact on the web. Or, you can read more about our services here.

Notice how this example uses natural, everyday human language to explain the development process. Any potentially confusing terms for non-technical people ("SEO", "responsiveness") are explained simply, as well. Clients don't understand code, design theory, or the implications of an improperly configured Apache server – always speak human language with clients. The above example can also be easily converted into talking points when you're conducting in-person or email communication.

Your processes are what make you financially valuable. Explaining them illustrates your unique skillset.

Common Freelancer Pricing Questions/Objections

By now, you might be thinking, "Yeah, that's nice and all, but you were talking about a $100,000 deal with an enterprise company. I'm one person without a lot of industry clout right now." Good point. Let's go through some

41

common freelancer questions and objections when it comes to pricing schemes.

"I'm new. I can't charge $3,000 for a website yet and expect people pay me for it...Can I?"

If you have a portfolio of previous work that explicitly shows the value you've created, there's no reason you can't charge $3,000 (or whatever number seems big to you right now) for a site that adds value to clients.

Again, it **always** comes back to this: *you need to know, in as explicit detail as possible, the value you're adding when you provide a service.*

You need to communicate this value to your client.

Undercharging is often a confidence issue rather than due to lack of expansive web tech skills: even freelance HTML developers make good money when they know the value they create. And remember, if you don't possess a certain tech or business skill, you can always learn it or outsource it.

"I live in an expensive country/state and can't compete in a global economy where $3/hr fullstack web developer college kids are rewarded."

Race-to-the-bottom freelance sites attract the worst clients, period.

Many times clients paying rock-bottom prices will:

- Demand excessive revisions
- Want additions outside the agreed-upon scope of work (done for free or very cheaply)
- Nitpick
- Leave scathingly negative reviews for small, fixable mistakes
- Threaten to not pay you or don't pay at all
- Undermine your work
- Demand unreasonable accommodations

Of course, these things can and do also happen in situations where the client is paying more than the minimum possible price. However, it's sad to say, but a lot of people simply don't respect low-wage workers.

This is all to say that just because you see people coding for a dollar an hour doesn't mean that's any kind of standard for you. Cheap coders are often disrespected and dehumanized due to their fire-sale rates—perceived as transactional middlemen (leading clients to the cheapest price possible) instead of talented developers who add value. There are tens of thousands of clients desperate for quality work right now with plenty of money in their pockets. They don't want the cheapest option; they want *quality*. They also:

- Appreciate supporting the local community.
- Recognize the craft of frequent, meaningful communication whether by phone or email without a time-zone difference.
- Value the option of meeting in person to ensure you're not a bot or scam artist.

Cheap coders may live next door to you – if so, start gathering and emphasizing all your competitive advantages! You'll have many. For example: you're not just a coder; you're a problem solver.

Absolutely **do not** let cheap coders negatively influence you. **Do not** fall for the temptation to charge rock-bottom prices. This brand of developer is on an entirely different business model that's unsustainable, impractical, and emotionally unhealthy for your own career.

"Can't I just charge hourly? That seems a lot easier for everybody."

Charging hourly punishes people who work efficiently. What happens if you can code an app in five minutes? Do you charge them five dollars? That's a pricing death trap.

Additionally, charging hourly can encourage a sloppy work ethic and is rarely a reflection of value. (For example, why would a developer code a page in two hours when that same developer can slow down, take it easy, and charge for three hours instead?)

Charging per project and establishing prices based on value makes sense for you and your clients. However, there are some scenarios where hourly pricing *does* make sense, such as consultations and training sessions. Hourly pricing in these situations encourages your client to keep things on-topic: when it costs a client $30, $50, or $100+ an hour to meet with you, there's not a lot of room for excessive sports score recaps and raving about the new sandwich at Chick-Fil-A.

"How do I know the value I'm adding before I've even met my client?"

If you're having a hard time deciding on what's appropriate to charge, do some investigative work on the competition in your area. What are they offering, what are they charging, and what can you do better to give yourself a competitive advantage?

Once you have your basics down ($1200 for a landing page; $300 to add an embedded contact form, etc.), then you can start determining additional prices that are relevant for each client when you discuss their business needs.

Exercise: Price Quote

In this exercise, you'll give a client a price quote for her project. Assume you have a website with a portfolio featuring similar real-world projects (in other words, you can handle her website needs and prove it if necessary).

Here's the scenario: A local business owner discovered your website and wants to discuss your services. She sent you an email, noting that she owns a successful dog walking business and wants a standard website (price listed on your site) with a custom reservation system built in. How much do you charge?

Take a few minutes to think about your pricing process in this scenario, then come back and read on.

The first part of the quote should be easy, since you already have a base price for a basic website published on your page: $1500. But what about the custom reservation system?

The first step to understanding (and conveying) the value of that service is to get to know your client's business better. After asking some questions, you find out she has over 4000 appointments per year with the dogs. The online reservation system would save her hundreds of hours each year, directing pre-payments right to her bank account, while opening up more slots for additional animals.

How does that information influence your quote?

Think about the value you can add with your custom system. Do you have a price in mind? How would you emphasize the benefits of your system to your client?

Again, take a few minutes to play out this scenario in your head (or better yet, have a friend play the role of the client).

Selling Your Services with PAR

Here's how I would respond to this client (notice how I'm using a PAR statement even on the phone):

"...Based on what you've told me, it sounds like you have a really robust business! But it also sounds like the admin tasks are really eating up your time." **[problem]**

"The best part is that this site and reservation system would be totally self-contained. I can develop it so that customers can easily pick their day, reserve the time, pay you, the money goes right into your account, and you get a notification on your devices when a reservation is made." **[action]**

"A website with a system like this could save you dozens of hours each week, and it would draw in new customers who use the web to search for local dog walkers. Also, you'd have additional time slots for walks since you're not doing admin stuff all the time. It really has the potentially of pulling a lot of money for you. I'd say probably most of your income within the first year would be drawn from the site." **[result]**

(Client approves of all these awesome ideas and results throughout the pitch, suggests more neat features she envisions, asks some follow-up questions along with how much it costs)

"...So, it's something to think about; I really think this could be a great asset to your business. And I'm personally really excited about this project because there's just so much growth potential and from what you've told me, it sounds like you really have pride in your company." **[building rapport]**

"With these benefits we just talked about, we're looking at around $4500, and with that you would also get three revisions along with a two-week turnaround time, and a one-hour in-person brainstorm session with you before we start developing. Also, all of our designs are responsive, so that means whether your customers are on mobile devices, laptops, desktops – whatever device they're on, the can access your site and your system with zero issues. My team and I focus on one project at a time, so these next two weeks is solely dedicated to your business and making it absolutely perfect." **[competitive advantage while explaining development process]**

(Rest of call is spent handling client objections, answering questions, etc.)

"I'm going to send you an email detailing what we just talked about – you can look over it at your convenience, take a look over all the benefits this new system has. And I'll check in with you on Wednesday if that works for you?" **[giving freedom to client, but maintaining control of timeline]**

Raising Prices

You may find yourself needing to raise your prices. Maybe you skill up, or you find yourself with more business confidence; perhaps you're coding more efficiently, or your cost of living went up – the reasons are numerous. I find email works best for this, as it gives clients time to absorb the message and respond appropriately, all while motivating them to get more work in so they can lock in your current rate rather than the increased rate.

```
Hi Rachel,

I wanted to take a moment to thank you for your business
over the past five months. I've really enjoyed working
with you and it's been very exciting seeing your
business grow and succeed!

Currently, I've been charging $40 per dev hour; however,
as of August 1st, 2019, my price per dev hour will
increase to $50. This price change will let me to offer
a more valuable and personalized service which, as a
result, will help you achieve greater results for your
business.

If you're anticipating any upcoming work, you can lock
in the current rate now. However, any new work booked on
or after August 1st will be charged at my new rate.

I appreciate you understanding and I look forward to
continuing our work together!
-Paulo
```

Pricing is difficult as a new freelancer. There are no hard and fast rules, no set-in-stone numbers, and people have varying pricing criteria. You'll often find yourself asking, "Is that too high?" or "Maybe I should raise my prices a little bit," or maybe even tempted to undervalue your services just to get some client buzz.

The good news is, nothing is permanent (especially true as a beginner), so you can always raise or lower your prices to find a sweet spot. The other good news is, once you get more experience, you will undoubtedly be able to charge more – experience has value, too.

Chapter Summary

This chapter gave you some ideas on how to start pricing your services. The most consistent and sustainable way of charging your clients as a newbie is based on **value, per project**. Hourly pricing is usually a death trap, unless you're dealing directly with clients via consultations and training. In those situations, the hourly rate encourages you and your client to stay on-topic.

In the next section, we're going to discuss "starter clients": critical people who allow you to eventually charge good money for these services.

Chapter 6

Starter Clients

In 2015, I was living in Minneapolis, Minnesota and studying the basics of programming and information technology while working on my Masters in Public Policy.

I was too new to land a tech job, didn't have the credentials to be a policy wonk for the government, and I needed money. So, I did what any other self-deprecating individual does: I went to work nights at the United States Postal Service.

For eight to twelve hours a night, my job was scan packages on a conveyer belt using a knuckle scanner and throw them into one of five containers. Because the job was mind-numbingly simple, I was able to work while having ample brain space to think and dream about nearly anything.

One night, as the latest clump of packages were inching towards me on the belt, I saw a picture in my mind. It was a promotional poster of a business...MY business. This business would offer digital services including photo, video, web design, blog services, and other things I was good at. The poster kept getting more and more vivid as I envisioned working on projects I enjoyed...for people I enjoyed.

But then a critical question popped in my mind: "How can people even know I'm legit if they don't know me?"

As I mindlessly clicked the knuckle scanner to process more packages, the answer popped into my mind like an answer to a trivia question: *Starter clients.*

Starter clients would be my primary key to building a portfolio, vouching for me, and allowing me to test my skills to prove myself. Working in a warehouse basement was not a place I saw myself for the rest of my life, not to mention for the next six months. I had a rough plan, an escape, a dream, and I was getting excited.

What Are Starter Clients and Why Do I Need Them?

Starter clients are your very first clients. They get you started in the industry.

They are real people with web needs and a big transition from personal projects and other "closed system" and/or theoretical development. They breathe, they eat, and they need websites. You need starter clients for a few reasons:

- Starter clients let you engage in all the proceedings of an official business transaction as a freelancer without many of the risks. You can sign contracts, you can develop a custom full-stack web app for them, you can write the documentation, and if you mess something up with any of that, your client is usually much more understanding than full-price clients. They know you're a beginner and trust you to make it right. In other words, they probably aren't going to head to your Facebook page and leave you a one-star review because you have to troubleshoot an email server and it's taking longer than you expected.

- Starter clients are your beta testers. They let you practice your communication skills, exercise your process-oriented thinking techniques, build and test your web development skills (sure, you know CSS, but can you implement it for somebody per their design specification?), and you have the opportunity to ask them for feedback every step of the way.

- Starter clients are filled with great things to say about you. Since they come from your networks, it's easier to solicit some truly wonderful feedback from them. This highly valuable positive feedback (social proof) should be used on your promotional materials, from posters to business cards to your own website.

- Starter clients are filled with great things to say about you to **others**. They can be a lucrative source for referrals.

- Starter clients let you build a real-world portfolio to showcase to full-paying clients.

Starter clients are all around you and serve as a gateway to full-price, real-world freelancing.

How Do I Find Starter Clients?

Starter clients can be found in your family, in your online and offline social networks, elsewhere on the web, on the streets...They're everywhere. Ask yourself: *Who needs a website, and who will trust me to build their website as a newbie?*

I found four starter clients using two avenues:

1. **My family.** They have a large offline social network (my parents own their own small business where they meet hundreds of new people every week) and once I made the announcement to them, they made the announcement to others. Through this group I made three stater clients, including a local non-profit.

2. **My own campaign.** I simply approached people I liked, who ran business I liked, and asked if they needed a website or digital marketing services for a ridiculously low cost. I secured a grocery store as a starter client using this method. In exchange, I received a huge wicker basket filled with grocery items and homemade treats.

Importantly, I wasn't billing myself as a super-experienced web developer or digital marketing guru to my network. Instead, I was honest about being new to the career field without being self-deprecating: I worked my butt off to be in this field and was pushing hard to succeed! I was happy share my journey up to this point. I also had a public portfolio of personal projects, so they could view my capabilities if they had reservations about my talents and abilities.

How Much Do I Charge Starter Clients?

With starter clients, there's an expectation that you're freshly minted as an independent web developer. In other words, they're usually not expecting the digital version of the Mona Lisa right off the bat. You're still in learning mode, and you're sure to make lots of mistakes and corrections during the development process. This is the place to do it! Experiments, ample A/B tests, note-taking, and other behavior designed to build your budding business come with the territory.

At the same time, you're doing your best to ensure this person has an awesome web package when you're done with it. They'll eventually get the keys to a shiny, new website with all the fixins. So what do your starter clients owe you for this?

Honestly?

Nothing.

...Zilch...

...Nada.

Maybe $300 at the most. Consider this: your starter clients are enabling you to build a *real-world portfolio*. This portfolio will be the basis for paying clients, who will also be the first people to write the major checks, leave great reviews, and tell other people about you. Indirectly, your starter clients are responsible for every cent you make as a freelancer. Don't you think you should cut them a super deal? I do.

For my own starter clients, I charged anywhere from $15 to $150 just to make sure they had a financial investment of some sort – any sort – in order to keep things on track. Even if it's a really small amount, both freelancer and client tend to be more attentive to communication and deadlines when a dollar sign is attached.

My work was high-quality and inexpensive, it was clear I cared about doing a good job, and people appreciated that. My first non-profit actually brought me a gift card for the local diner along with some other swag for their appreciation. Another starter client slipped me some extra cash as a tip. It may seem like you're in a bubble while behind the computer screen for 8 to 16 hours a day, but you really are helping people achieve their goals and dreams with your work. Starter clients are no exception.

Interviewing Your Starter Clients So You Can Solve Their Problems

Fortune tellers are in a very compelling career field, but unfortunately for us freelancers, it's hard for us to read minds. When somebody approaches you and says, "I need a website for my law firm," the first thing you most definitely **don't** do is hop onto the nearest laptop, fire up a local copy of WordPress, and code out a landing page. You have no idea what they actually want on the site. So, instead of rubbing your temples and straining your brain for a vision, you start asking questions:

"What type of law firm is this? Tell me more about your business."

"What are your goals with this site? Are you trying to source clients, or is this site more part of a brand-awareness campaign?"

"What do you want the site to look like? Do you have brand assets?"

The list goes on. The more specific questions you ask, the more specific answers you'll get, which gives you excellent insight into your upcoming site design.

Sitting down with your client for an interview gives you major insight into their tech needs.

But this is more than just a Q&A session; this is an **interview**, giving you the opportunity to deeply explore the needs and vision your starter client has. (The word "interview" can be intimidating for some people, so I usually just use the world "chat" when setting up a meet time.)

Conduct your interviews with your starter clients wherever you both feel most comfortable, whether it's at the local diner or a Skype session. In this case, your starter clients are often friends or family members (or other high-trust individuals), so inviting them over for a chat and a coffee could work nicely, too.

Not sure where to start with the interview? Follow these steps for guidance:

0. **Pre-Interview.** Don't go to the interview cold, but rather collect as much information on this person and their business before the interview as you can. Have a list of questions ready to go.

1. **Actively Listen.** This goes beyond nodding your head and saying "Mmmhmm" to your starter client's voice—with active listening, you're writing things down, processing information, absorbing the whole story, and thinking of follow-up questions to ask as this person shares her ideas.

2. **Re-Direct the Interview.** This is totally new territory for your interviewee, and many times the conversation gets derailed. Gently re-direct the interview when things get off topic so you can continue to extract the information you need to make the perfect website for this person.

3. **Feed Information Back.** There's a lot being shared at this interview. Read back what your client told you, allowing this person to essentially proofread your notes about the project. She'll correct you when something sounds wrong and add info when something sounds ambiguous.

4. **"Is There Anything Else You'd Like to Add?"** This is my final question before wrapping up the interview. In my experience, this question consistently brings the most insightful answers and often brings up a whole new conversation about the client's true vision.

Chapter Summary

Starter clients are your VIPs and MVPs. They enable you to build a portfolio based on real-world projects that create real-world value for entities ranging from non-profits to small businesses. This portfolio is the basis for virtually every cent you earn as a freelancer. Treat your starter clients like the true VIPs and MVPs they are, and you'll not only be helping people who want you to succeed, you'll also be setting yourself up for referrals from this first batch of customers.

You've got your starter clients down; now let's talk about more clients...The full-paying kind.

Chapter 7

Finding More Clients

Although I know a lot of people, my inner circle is pretty small. So, when I was started my own freelance career, I researched a *lot* about how to find clients. Most of the materials suggested that I rely on paid search (along with advanced SEO tactics, which can take months to years to show results), including buying strategic Facebook and Google AdWords ads to promote my services. Guess what?

It didn't work.

At. All.

It was a total time and money drain, even after I did my research. These techniques can work wonderfully when you're more established – but they hardly ever work when you're starting out.

Why?

Because **beginners have a low trust-factor**. Remember, the internet is a no-trust platform, and unfortunately, as newbies we're relegated to the bottom of the barrel when it comes to trust and confidence with strangers.

I also spent a lot of my time emailing and calling website-less strangers. They didn't tell me this in the books, but what I was doing was actually a spam campaign.

- Unsolicited contact for a product I never even used? **Check**.

- Offering services to strangers for a fee? **Check**.

- Following up with more emails and calls despite the lack of interest from the other party? **Check**.

It's no wonder my success rate was exactly zero. I had to get better at this – I had to get people to *trust me*. As it turns out, the answer was right in front of my face.

Family and Friends as Recruiters: Your Number One Weapon

We make things so convoluted sometimes.

I had just spent my hard-earned money on a failed ad campaign; emailed and called the living hell out of local and out-of-town businesses that didn't have websites; worked diligently to get my outbound link game on point; and put my heart into trying to convince others that their lack of responsive web design principles on their pre-existing site was going to be their personal nuclear apocalypse.

A flood of negative and borderline-ridiculous thoughts circled in my head:

Maybe I sound desperate, too passive-aggressive?

Maybe it's because I'm a female?

I'm definitely too nerdy.

Obviously, I picked the wrong career field because nobody wants to freakin' hire me.

I was ready to transition to some other career field altogether because I had exhausted my resources. (No, seriously. I wanted to go back to graphic design or perhaps finally put my MPP (Masters of Public Policy) to use.)

A couple days later, I got a call from my dad, who owns an antiques and collectibles store. "I was talking a couple who came in today. They own that little motel down the road."

I sighed. That place was notorious for its slummy accommodations and I knew any story involving it was nothing but trouble.

"They just bought it, brand new owners. Said they're doing a complete remodel and want to make give it a real nice up-north cabin feel for the snowmobilers and fishermen. I told them you do websites if they need one."

He proceeded to give me the new owners' phone number. Score!

Our conversation reminded me that I "went public" with my new foray into freelance web development:

I made the announcement at family get-togethers.

I made the announcement on social media.

I made the announcement to anybody who would stumble on my website.

At any sort of gathering where I had one-on-one communication with people, I made the announcement and talked more about it. How building websites was not just a hobby anymore, but my career.

I also passively made the announcement in my hometown, plastering business cards on boards inside the lobbies of independently-owned businesses I frequented, where people stopping to read would recognize my name.

The importance of announcing to your family, friends, acquaintances, and professional network that you're now doing freelancing cannot be emphasized enough. **These are the people who love you, believe in you, and want you to succeed.** They're going to bring you leads with the massive benefit of a built-in trust factor. You're not a stranger to the client anymore – you're Ricki's daughter, or Ralph's nephew, or Raul's friend, or Manja's recommendation.

With these clients, you're not a zero-trust-factor service provider with a glossy pay-per-click ad campaign; you're somebody trustworthy who can solve their highly-technical problems.

Your local network will start working for you once you put the word out, but it does take patience. Don't give up when hordes of familiar faces aren't pounding on your apartment door demanding websites! I thought it worked like that early in my career, and felt discouraged when people weren't contacting me immediately. The process takes time and starts as a trickle. Trust the process.

Be bold in your announcements, be proactive in social media, and weave your new career path into every conversation where it seems appropriate.

You will find yourself repeating yourself often, but that's a good thing, as long as you don't turn into a human spam-bot where that's *all* you talk about.. The idea is to have people associate you with web development expertise. When they need services, or when they're talking with somebody in their circle about business development, your name should be hoisted the top of their brain's execution stack. Do the math: if you hammer home your new profession to twenty people who each know twenty people, that's potentially 400 people who know about you and what you do. Then multiply that group of 400 people by twenty people and...you get the idea. You're going viral in the analog world.

To summarize this section, the easiest way to find full-paying clients as a new freelancer is through your local network. That built-in trust factor has the priceless benefit that no other advertising method can match.

Referrals Are the Best Clients That Keep Giving and Giving

Here's what's brilliant about freelancing. Once you've impressed a few good (good = pleasant and paying) clients with your impeccable communication skills, your gorgeous designs, and fast, killer features delivered in a timely fashion, they're going to talk about you. They'll talk about you to their friends and family, their business acquaintances, and even *their* clients. Good clients tend to stick with their own kind, so if they're sending somebody your way, there's a good chance they'll also be the type of client you want to deal with.

Going viral with good clients is the best thing that can happen in your freelancing career. Referrals bring in more referrals. It requires zero advertising dollars, saves you lots of time, and consistently brings in money. It also makes your job infinitely more enjoyable when compared to tougher or hard-sell clients.

Engage Freelancer Mode! Opportunities Are *Everywhere*

It doesn't matter if I'm just talking a stroll downtown or out on a road trip. Every time I see a building with a business sign on it, I take note: What is it? How long have they been here and who owns this place? Do they have a website? Sometimes I'll take a photos or a quick video of the sign to research more when I get home.

I love a good flea market, and you can find me exploring the booths that feature anything vintage and unusual. On my way to the next booth, I'll scoop up the vendor's business card and explore later what kind of online presence they have, if any. It's easy to collect ten, twenty, and even more business cards at these events.

Any time I go to my bank, coffeeshop, greasy spoon diner, or thrift store, I scour the announcement board where people post upcoming events — they also post business cards and personal flyers. Any piece of advertising that doesn't have a website gets my immediate attention.

See where this is going? When I'm out and about, my freelance mindset is *activated*. It's to the point where I don't even think of these activities anymore — it's totally non-cerebral, just like putting on a seat belt is when I get in a car. Whether it's shopping for vinyl records or browsing a thrift store, the freelancer in me is automatically engaged, and always open to new possibilities, connections, and clients.

It's up to you to engage your own freelancer mindset. At first, it might seem weird looking around your own neighborhood like a tourist, eyes darting in all directions, soaking up the information. You might feel out of place by walking up to small town gift shop and taking a picture of its marquee for later reference. A lot of this takes some getting used to, but once you get into the habit, you'll find yourself seeing business opportunities you've never seen before, instinctively snatching up business cards at places you frequent, and otherwise having your freelance antennae tuned into the world around you.

Target-Rich Environments

Some places are more lucrative than others when it comes to finding leads. Here are some target-rich environments where I have had repeated success:

Grocery Stores & Food Markets. This includes corner stores, meat markets, bodegas, farmer's markets, co-ops, independently-owned grocers, as well as larger chain grocery stores. Grocery stores are target-rich because they have (tens of) thousands of products. You can really strike it rich with locally-produced products, although I've also found a few companies with regional and national distribution that are still without websites. For some odd reason, the spice aisle has been particularly target-rich for me. Also, the store itself may be in need of a website or site revamp. Online ordering and home delivery is a big deal these days, and can be huge selling points as a web developer. Ecommerce is also more financially valuable than a static website, and thousands of products can be sold via ecommerce at these venues. In other words: this category can make you some good money!

Food vendors are very target-rich. They not only sell numerous products that need websites; the vendor herself often needs a website along with other digital services.

Flea Markets & Expos. This includes arts and crafts shows along with trade shows. Basically, any place with a large group of independent vendors who own small businesses. If they don't own a small business yet, a website could be just the thing they need to get bring their operation to the next level. Observe how people operate, take note of their inventory, notice their communication style and note anything else about how they do business. All these observations can be used to craft the perfect sales pitch down the road (we'll talk about this further in the chapter).

Yellow Pages. Remember when phone books used to look like...phone books? Nowadays, they're about the length of a Teen Vogue magazine. Despite their drastic downsizing since the expansion of the web, the yellow pages can be a gold mine for client leads. Even better, businesses in the yellow pages are broken down by industry, an indispensable feature if you're doing niche work or want to avoid certain industries altogether.

Want to Land that Contract? Treat People Like They're Already Clients

You might not realize it, but throughout your day-to-day activities, you're building rapport with people at restaurants, convenience stores, hobby and game shops, and wherever else you find yourself. These are also excellent opportunities to share what you do. Here's a technique that I use that's seen great results.

I bought about a dozen USB sticks online, making sure they had key rings on them. I put my portfolio and some positive blurbs about my work on the stick as an HTML file along with a PDF. I then put a punch hole through my business card, and threaded the card onto the stick: voila! A "business card plus" with a mobile portfolio. Whenever I went out, especially at good restaurants (it's one of my niches and I'm also an obsessive foodie), I would hand out one of my sticks to the manager on duty and sometimes the owner if he or she was around. Whoever the decision maker or major influencer was on duty, I sought him out. The thing was, most of these people already knew me because I was a regular at these places.

Usually it would go something like this:

Me to server after I paid the bill: "My soup was delicious. Is the owner here by chance? I need to give him this." (dangling USB)

Server: "Actually no, the owner isn't really here all that often."

Me: "OK, is Thanh around?" (server points to shift manager)

Me: "Thanh! I loved the bone marrow in the pho broth tonight. It was divine. Anyway, I was trying to check out your guys' online menu the other night and noticed you don't have a website...Just a Facebook page. I might have told you this before, but I'm a web developer and I specialize in websites for restaurants. Full menu uploads, a photo gallery of some of your best items, online ordering – we've got to get you going with this website thing." (*conversation continues: check this thing out, I'll find you next time I'm here, OK great, see you*)

If people aren't sold by your pitch, a free USB stick will help get them there. It shows them that you've already invested in them before they've even become your customer. Everybody likes feeling special, and this is one inexpensive way to show potential clients that you've gone out of your way to invest in them. You're showing that you value them, even before you've started talking serious business.

Potential clients love this technique – and again, it's built on a platform of trust. You're a familiar face to this person and the conversation feels natural. This person feels additionally valued because while talk is cheap, USB sticks are not.

Thoughtful trinkets like USB sticks show clients that you've already invested in them.

You don't have to use USBs to drive your message home. Think of other knick-knacks or out-of-the-ordinary actions that will make the clients in their respective niches feel valued. For example, if your niche is boating, what about a cool custom floating keychain with your business info and portfolio link printed on it? If you *really* want to make an impression, print "Property Of" followed by that specific business' name on the flip side.

Start Collecting Positive Feedback Right Away

Before I go to a new restaurant, I read the reviews.

Before I hit that "Add to Cart" button on Amazon for a new exotic spice, I read the reviews.

I mean, I read the reviews before doing almost *everything*. Over the years, I've walked blindly into situations where I've lost lots of money along with my appetite. It's just not worth it anymore. So, before I try something new that involves financial investment, I log on and see what others are saying.

Now multiply me times two or three billion. People who are online read reviews because it helps them make a more informed decision about how to spend their time and money. These same people want to read reviews about **you**.

Start collecting positive feedback and endorsements wherever you can from clients – even if it's Mom or Dad. Some people call it social proof. I use a simple spreadsheet to collect mine and it works nicely. It also has the benefit of boosting your mood when you're having a bad day. Consult your database of kind words and plaster some on your website (as discussed in Chapter 3). You can also sprinkle some positive feedback on your marketing materials like business cards.

These brief endorsements are crucial to employ wherever possible. They emphasize your trust factor to clients, lend to your credibility as a professional, and humanize your businesses. One day soon, people will be reading Yelp and Google reviews about *you*. Don't be shy with sprinkling this feedback wherever you can – being modest and concealing the awesome things people say about you just doesn't make sense in this business.

Getting Creative (Guerrilla Marketing)

Creative thinking can always make you money, and creative thinking in client acquisition is no different. I use a bunch of different non-traditional techniques in finding new clients, some of which have been very lucrative. Most of those efforts have centered on *guerrilla marketing*.

Guerrilla marketing is designed to be executed on the street or other public place, and involves little to no marketing budget. I love guerrilla marketing, mostly because it allows me to be creative with my business while giving people a smile or making their day a little more interesting.

Guerrilla marketing is unconventional, street-level advertising.

The absolute best guerrilla marketing strategy I've witnessed was when I was a full-time musician and CDs were still the big thing. I was walking outside a popular music store one summer afternoon and all the sudden something shimmery and rainbow-tinted caught my eye in the parking lot...First one, then two, then twenty or more. They were CDs!

My stomach jumped with excitement as I walked fast to pick them up before somebody else snatched them. "Must've fallen out of somebody's bag," I said to myself, "...Lucky me!"

As I picked one up, anticipating a killer album as I flipped it over, I saw that it wasn't a CD...*But a CD-shaped flyer for an upcoming album release.* Yes, some company using guerrilla marketing tactics got me to flip over their fake CD to inform me of their artist's upcoming album because they knew music lovers go ape over free music, especially right outside a music store when they're feeling pumped and ready to rock.

You might not get very good results throwing floppy disks on busy sidewalks with your name and website on them (then again, it might work really well!), but think about cheap or free ways you can get your name out on the street. What about handbills you design like the old '60s psychedelic posters stapled to popular ad boards and utility poles? Or dressing up in a chicken suit handing out plastic Easter eggs with a mini-business card and small prize inside, shaking a tail feather down Main Street in the afternoon? Keep it legal, have fun, and remember that while these things may sound silly, the idea is to stand out from the crowd while delivering a business message.

Guerrilla marketing requires zero marketing budget, aside from incidentals such as printing expenses and the like.

Upwork, Fiverr, Other Hire-A-Freelancer Sites

I highly discourage you from offering your services on global freelancing platforms like Upwork and Fiverr in order to find quality clients.

Can you use these sites? Absolutely.

Will you make a living from these sites? Probably not.

These popular freelancing sites are a global gathering of those who charge the least money possible for their services. Not only is this a race to the bottom, it's also unsustainable for those who don't live in developing countries and other places where the cost of living is low. It's also a huge time drain because your proposal is in the mix with dozens of others competing for the same job. You end up spending a **lot** of time on proposals that never make it out of the heap.

Some may argue that you can use these sites to build your portfolio – and that's true, you can – but why risk the potential negative reviews, excessive client demands, and borderline-abusive client emails that are common in low-wage sites when you can build sites for friends and family who need them? You also have the handicap of being new, so unless you devise a scheme for your acquaintances to hire you on these sites and leave positive feedback, you'll have a zero trust factor with no social proof.

Of course, you're absolutely free to experiment with these sites as a service provider. Odds are, however, you'll find it a waste of time and energy, and it'll end up being a *huge* opportunity cost. Think about all that time spent crafting those $150 proposals on Upwork when you could've been working quality leads in your own networks. Greener pastures certainly await you, even as a newbie.

Chapter Summary

While tempting, there's no need to reinvent the wheel by searching for clients in far away places using novel techniques or running an ad campaign: your own networks of friends, family, acquaintances, along with your public encounters will provide a treasure trove of leads. By far the biggest benefit of these leads is that there is a trust factor inherent in every encounter. Rather than a stranger with an advertising budget and cute headshot, you're a familiar face who builds high-quality websites and delivers results. As a newbie, this is your secret weapon.

Chapter 8

The Name Game

Getting your name out there is a critical part of building your business, specifically when it comes to building trust with clients. This is the earliest stage of marketing, and you should take advantage of all the free and inexpensive outlets you come across. You may not get any callbacks from a Craigslist ad, Facebook group post, or a signature block on a coding forum, but these low-level marketing efforts plant a seed in peoples' minds that you're affiliated with freelance web development and emphasize your professional image. Your ads and blurbs don't have to be million-dollar Super Bowl commercial contenders, but you should take time to create (or hire somebody to create) materials that succinctly capture what you do and why people need you.

Here's an example of a simple, effective local Craigslist ad. Remember, the goal isn't exclusively to get clients, but to also push brand awareness to the public in your local area.

(Title) Web developer now taking new clients – Ask about our special CraigsList rates!

(Body) Most sites are built with the purpose of "getting on the web." But getting online doesn't mean you're getting results: it just means you have a few pages floating around on the Internet. Meanwhile, your competition is sponging up all that valuable traffic.

Hi, I'm Candy. As an experienced web developer specializing in small businesses development in the Orlando area, it's my job to create fast, beautiful, and feature-rich ecommerce websites that put your competition to shame. My focus is giving you not just a website, but an active digital presence that gets *results*.

Traffic.

Clicks.

Conversions.

Happy customers who smile when their package arrives.

You know, all that good stuff that drives the heart of your online business.

I work with a small team of technical and creative professionals who are dedicated to their craft. With their vision and skills, we also offer the following services:

- Web design
- Video and photo packages
- Graphic Design
- Logo Design/Rebranding
- Copywriting
- SEO services
- Cloud hosting

A Facebook page serving as your main digital presence just doesn't cut it these days. Call the RealToughCandy.com office here in Orlando (407-555-5555) or send me an email today and let's discuss how we can take your business to the next level. If you already have a site, be sure to ask about my free SEO audit!

Cheers,
Candy

P.S. You can check out my portfolio here.

Remember to add photos of your logo, screenshots from projects, and any marketing flyers or other digital materials to your ad:

You can easily convert this type of post for social media usage, too.

Traditional Marketing as a Newbie: Mostly A Money Pit

I have to be honest here: when I was working on the outline of this book, I reviewed my theoretical chapters and said, "Wait, I don't have a marketing chapter. I suppose I should watch that *Complete Digital Marketing Course* again on Udemy and come back and report my findings."

It was tempting for a few reasons. Fist of all, what beginning freelancer wants to be told that traditional marketing doesn't help them? Secondly, it seemed foolish to not include a chapter that tells people how to advertise in a way everybody else talks about.

But after much debate, I decided it would be even *more* foolish to advise you to advertise in ways that aren't going to help you as a newbie. Over the years, I've met dozens of freelance web developers and whenever I ask them about their success with AdWords, targeted Facebook ads, and paying for SEO rankings boosts, *none* of them had success as beginners. None! As somebody who's blown through $100 a week in targeted Facebook ads as a newbie, these campaigns just do not deliver for the average newbie freelancer. Why? Because **it takes months, and sometimes even years, to secure your trust factor**. In other words, people don't trust complete strangers with little experience. It takes months – and even years – to get that one golden endorsement by an influential client that convinces strangers you're worth their investment. It takes months and even years for you to get your global SEO game on point with your blog titles, content, and photos, steering global Internet traffic your way.

For these reasons, traditional marketing as a beginning web developer is usually a money pit. It's best to stick to the low-hanging and bountiful fruit of your network: friends, family, associates, daily human encounters, forums and other online hubs where you're a member, Meetup opportunities, and similar homegrown efforts. People who believe in you are going to talk about you to their own networks, creating a viral network where quality leads create more quality leads.

The Exception: Ranking for Local SEO

If it's one effort in this department that may be worth your while as a newbie, it's ranking for local SEO. By this, I mean targeting your site so it attracts local online traffic and appears on the first page of search results.

For example, if you lived in Charleston, South Carolina and somebody Google'd "Web developer Charleston," your website would be one of the first to display. Aside from increasing your trust factor being a fellow local, many people also like staying local for civic reasons, such as supporting their community and putting their money into the local economy.

You don't have to pay anybody to start ranking for local SEO, but it can take some time to rank. Also, SEO is a *massive* topic and there are dozens of ways you can rank your website. I wouldn't necessarily prioritize learning about these methods as a newbie (remember, low-hanging fruit come first), but you may be looking at a whole new segment of clients from around your local area.

It's certainly worth researching more if you're ready to expand your client roster. As mentioned above, the *Complete Digital Marketing Course* on Udemy by Rob Percival and Daragh Walsh is a good starting point; take what you can use. Daragh dedicates over three hours to SEO techniques, with a 23-minute lecture specifically dedicated to local SEO.

Exercise

Write a Craigslist ad for your freelance business. While the main purpose is to establish name recognition, also be open to legitimate customer interest in your services (but do be critical and careful when it comes to responses to your ad – good people are out there, but there are lots of spammers. Don't rush anything, never disclose personal info, and always research the person as best you can).

In the ad, answer the basics of who you are and what you do while emphasizing how you can solve your potential clients' most common problems. Be sure to include a call to action - "Call me today," etc. (Hint: Use the information in your business plan to shape the tone of the ad.)

Chapter 9

Customer Service (Still Matters)

We live in an era of self-checkout kiosks, online bill pay systems, and automatic car washes with Muppet-looking apparatuses caressing our vehicles. Many of us even go days without interacting with strangers – it's never been easier to live in a bubble. In fact, isolation is rewarded a lot in society! Add this to the fact that many web developers are introverts: as a result, interacting with customers can be a very socially awkward experience.

On the other hand, perhaps you've had previous experience in customer service, and know what it takes to instill confidence in customers and proactively handle unexpected issues.

Either way, *customer service still matters*. People notice how they're treated and they then share that experience. When you first start freelancing, how these people respond to your treatment is going to set the tone for your career. Let's take a look at some focus areas where you might improve your customer service efforts.

The Difference Between Good Experiences and Bad Ones

Here's what clients value during – and after – the development process:

- ✓ Honest communication
- ✓ A positive attitude
- ✓ Progress updates when things are going right
- ✓ Status updates when things are going wrong
- ✓ A walkthrough of their new site
- ✓ A quality website delivered on time and to specification

All pretty basic stuff, right? You'd be surprised how easy it is to do these things below standard. Lots of developers make promises they can't keep, rarely give updates, and many don't even have their heart in their projects.

Clients notice.

This is your chance to really outshine your competition: if you can master these basics, if you can drive your concentration into that person's project, it'll show. There's a good chance your client is going to value not only your work, but **you**. It means the difference between a client snatching their website from you, never seeing you again; and raving to their high-quality network while peppering the web with positive reviews about your business.

Neutralizing a Poor Attitude

After years of interacting with clients and other freelancers, I've seen so many instances where freelancers fail because of bad attitudes...Including myself.

We are all liable to become annoyed after a client's fourth – and most likely unnecessary – revision request.

We are all liable to become frustrated because clients don't understand that things can go wrong when we tweak server configuration files.

We all have bad days, and sometimes it's hard to separate our home life from our work life.

It's easy to let your emotions slip into the business domain, but we have to neutralize these surges. Deep breathe. Take a walk, explore nature, hit the gym. Drink a coffee or tea and blast some music. Do what you can to get in a better state of mind, because bad attitudes are one of *the* fastest ways to find yourself out of business as a new freelance developer. You may be antisocial by default, your favorite type of company may be the glowing orb of your laptop at three in the morning, but no matter what – you **must** have a positive attitude with clients, even when (especially when) you don't want to. It's a non-negotiable item. Remember, **your job is to solve problems for people** – not make them worse.

Even in the tech era, we're all still people. Our brains haven't been implanted with chips yet, and we're still free to make independent decisions. Clients experience the same feelings and thoughts as those in the olden days did, and want to be treated with respect, empathy, and professionalism.

You also have the additional burden of neutralizing situations that may make a turn for the worse, and transforming them into bridge-building business deals. That's a tall order. But with practice, focus, and a positive attitude, you can overcome a bad mood and whatever other mental block so it doesn't spill over to your freelance career.

There's no substitute for good customer service, so if speaking to strangers in a professional capacity freaks you out, the solution is to practice, practice,

practice. Practice with friends and family with simulated business scenarios, practice at the drug store check-out, practice with your sushi chef, and it will get easier, even if that means going from "OMG, I can't talk to this person" to "OK, this might stink and I might stutter but I'll give it a shot."

Trust me, I know firsthand how crippling this anticipatory anxiety is. But most times once the interaction is over, I'm like, "Oh, OK. That went a lot better than I thought it would go. Sweet." Do you really want to know what gets me over the shyness and anxiety? I tell myself, "You know, I might die tomorrow and I'll definitely be dead in fifty years, tops. I should just go talk to this person." It's *super* morbid, but it's one of the only things that can get me over my anxiety a lot of times.

Dealing with Negative Feedback

Not going to lie, negative feedback still hurts. I tell myself people are having bad days; I tell myself I'm not perfect; I tell myself it happens to everyone. But when I see those one- and two-star reviews online, my stomach still sinks.

It doesn't matter if they are 100% in-your-face truthful, if they're exaggerated with some truths sprinkled throughout, or if they're completely fabricated: negative feedback sucks. And trust me, even if you're the best freelancer of all time, the Muhammed Ali of JavaScript, the Jimi Hendrix of WordPress, the Second Coming of Turing – **you will get negative feedback.** It stinks to high heaven, but it's part of the game.

The good news is that it happens to all of us – every freelancer can empathize with you when that client comes along convinced he knows how to code, then rates you two stars because you refused to let him touch the backend of the project during the build.

The bad news is...it's negative feedback.

While it may be tempting to immediately respond to these public criticisms, one-star reviews, and outright hate while you're ticked off – **don't.** It doesn't resolve anything, and for people who don't know you (which is almost everybody reading the review section), you come across as hotheaded and rude. People will go to another company where they don't feel as threatened.

Instead, take a day to cool off and analyze what type of person left the negative review:

- Was it a genuinely disappointed client?

- Was it possibly a competitor? (Hint: users with cryptic usernames and no photo who leave one-star reviews of your services are often competitors.)

- Was it somebody who benefitted from your services and enjoyed the process, but grades very strictly, is having an off-day, or is idiosyncratic? ("...Had to ding off two stars for not having fresh coffee at our final meeting")

- Was it an ex or somebody who has an issue with you personally and wants to see you fail?

After your analysis, proceed as follows:

If you received a poor feedback rating from a genuinely disappointed client or one who grades strictly:

Reply publicly with a sincere apology. Thank your customer for the honest feedback, apologize, and express how you're more than happy to to work with that client to fix whatever needs fixing. If it's a technical issue, fix that. If it's a communication issue, those are a little harder to remedy. Sometimes throwing in a free six months of an additional service (SEO auditing? Web Hosting? Something the client values) can help heal a jaded client. They're also more likely to come back and update their review when you fix their problem.

If you received a poor feedback rating from a bot, competitor, ex, or hater:

If you absolutely know it's bogus, you could offer them a full, 100% refund. This shows the public that you're serious about customer service and quality work, while you risk absolutely nothing. After all, 100% of nothing means you owe them exactly...nothing.

One other effective technique to neutralize this ratings scar is to screenshot the review and post it to your social media. People who follow you and know your work is quality will respond with encouragement, often going to the review page itself to give five-star reviews to "neutralize" the fake one-star review. Note that you're not actually asking your people to inflate the review site with five-star reviews about your business (because that's going into Questionable-Ethics Land). Many will do it on their own accord as a natural response, without prompting...And in that case, who's to stop them?

Check our how Joy Hawkins responded to a user named "Rocky Stallone" who dished out a fake one-star review for her business:

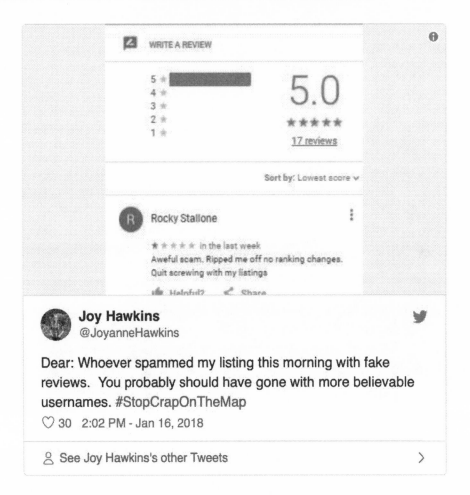

The important thing about dealing with negative feedback is to take a proactive approach, no matter if the review is real or fake. Responding to real negative reviews gives you a chance to fix the issues, grow your business, and build trust with clients; responding to fake negative reviews gives you a chance to exhibit your commitment to quality and excellent customer service to potential clients, even though it was spurred on by haters and fakes.

Chapter Summary

In this chapter, we covered how to implement quality customer service, a critical component to succeeding in freelance web development. Your reputation is the most important thing to protect and defend as a newbie. Next, we'll move on to the first technical component of sealing the business deal: proposals.

Chapter 10

The Proposal

You've answered your clients' questions, eased their concerns, and gave them the confidence they need to believe you're capable. Now comes the first major technical challenge. You need to create a document that outlines everything great you're going to do for them, while keeping it non-technical enough so they can understand it. Plus, you need to include all the juicy details of the deal minus the padding of gentle words on the phone: things like final price, delivery dates, and exact functions and features. Welcome to proposal land.

We'll keep this chapter brief and newbie-friendly. As a beginning freelancer, you likely won't be needing to draft 200-page novels that include executive outlines and the like (most of the proposals I wrote as a beginner were a few very short paragraphs). Here's an example proposal you could use with your own clients. Say this client needs a site for his law firm:

Project Objectives

Increasingly, users are visiting websites on mobile devices with a wide range of screen sizes. My team and I design all of my websites with mobile responsiveness mind. Your website will be modified to adapt and scale to any device. Additionally, those in need of law firm services are searching for accurate, timely information. This reality underscores the need for a blog area with a featured comment section to start a dialogue with you and your guests.

Finally, in order for more users to connect with you, they will also need expanded avenues to access your site. We will implement industry-standard, locally-targeted SEO techniques to open up a larger audience of potential clients.

Scope of Work

My team and I will develop website design concepts and migrate existing content to a website with the following features:
- Custom-designed, mobile-responsive website to match your branding, and represent the five-star experience of working with your law firm.

- Inviting call-to-action buttons that direct visitors to book an appointment or contact you.

- **Search Engine Optimization**: Pages are fully optimized for search engine visibility. This includes: Google MyBusiness listing. Page Speed Optimization. Keyword research and implementation.

- **Blog Creation**: A well-managed blog will improve local SEO results, as well as provide a valuable resource for site visitors. (We customize the CMS dashboard to make editing blog posts and pages easy for you.)

Timeline

We estimate this project will take six weeks to develop. More information on our exact development process can be found here:

www.freelanceLanceyPants.com/process

Your Investment

Total cost: $3200. The payment will be delivered in 3 installments as the project hits certain milestones:

1. $800 initial deposit to be paid before work begins.

2. $1000 paid after designs are approved. Custom development begins.

3. $1400 once the website is live.

If you have any questions or need additional information amended to the proposal, please let me know.

Once approved, I will contact you to schedule a project launch meeting to finalize everything and gather all necessary brand assets before beginning the project.

Thank you!

Blimpy LanceyPants, Owner & Lead Developer
www.freelanceLanceyPants.com

Not too crazy, right?

One thing to note is the timeline: it'll take an estimated six weeks to finish the project. I like to add a week to what I actually think it will take me to complete the project. This gives me a weeklong grace period if things go bad (lots of broken code, unexpected family or personal event, etc.). If things **do** go as planned, I get to hand over a shiny new website to my client *a whole week* before she expected it! That always makes clients happy and adds a lot to your reputation. The gurus call this the "**underpromise and overdeliver**" strategy. The idea is that you set a comfortable scope and timeline for your service, and then wow them by delivering the results ahead of time, possibly with some sort of "bonus" item (like additional contact form functionality, for example).

This entire proposal can be rolled into the final contract, saving you a lot of time. Let's go over that now.

Chapter 11

Writing That Contract

When I started out, the thought of drafting up a contract for my clients seemed pretentious. We were both adults, I had the talent and they had the money, and we agreed to my project.

This got me in trouble.

Every.

Single.

Time.

Contracts are more than just legally binding agreements. They gently remind the client they have to pay you, and they remind *you* that you have a website to build. It's a roadmap for the both of you.

With one exception – a local and long-established non-profit – I **never** got paid on time from my non-contract clients. **NEVER**. In fact, I waited over three months to get paid by one of them even after multiple reminders. Since nothing was in writing, it was also easier for clients to sneak in extra features ("Oh, this doesn't include a custom PDF-to-mp4 converter? I thought that was part of the deal?").

In retrospect, I wanted to believe my clients were flawless, upstanding people who respected not only my business, but me. *Why would somebody in my own town who was a referral from a family member exploit my talents?*

Whether intentional or not, freelancers *do* get exploited when a business deal is just a handshake at a coffeeshop or an agreement on the phone. And, as hard as it is for me to admit, I make mistakes, too. Developers misunderstand agreements, misinterpret requests, and engage in any number of other unintentional miscommunications. A contract solves these problems by establishing rules for both parties, and forces the client and freelancer to be on the same page.

Even if it's a friend of a friend or some other seemingly trustworthy referral, **always write a contract prior to starting work and make sure you and your client sign it**. Additionally, take a down payment before starting any work to ensure the client is serious about paying you. You also want to make sure there is a provision that reserves the right for you to showcase the site in your portfolio and other marketing materials.

Real-World Contract Templates/Examples

Jyssica Schwartz is a freelancer who open-sourced her own five-page no-nonsense contract. Feel free to use it: https://bit.ly/2xHFJ9f

Stuff & Nonsense published a popular open-source contract a few years ago. The language is more hipster-y than your standard contract fare, but it has a really nice human touch. Note use of British English spellings and edit if necessary: https://stuffandnonsense.co.uk/projects/contract-killer/

A Nerd's World has a very cool, distinct-looking contract that is short and human-readable: https://anerdsworld.com/wp-content/uploads/2018/07/anw_webcontract_updated.pdf

As mentioned in the previous chapter, you can integrate a lot (if not all) of your proposal wording into the contract. In my own contracts, I'll usually integrate my original proposal plus a terms and conditions section, including clauses on liability, revisions, additions, and my right to showcase the website. Again, **make sure you and your client sign and date this contract.** Otherwise, it's just another piece of paper and if something goes wrong, you won't have any legal recourse.

Practice: Drafting a Mock Contract

In this practice, you'll draft a mock contract.

The law firm client from the proposal in Chapter 10 wants to move forward. Using the above contract links as guides, write a suitable contract for the project. Proofread, ensuring everything is grammatically correct and makes sense from your client's standpoint.

Chapter 12

Developing

This is *your* freelance business, and you're doing things your way. Feels good, right? While you have total control over how you conduct yourself with your business matters, there are a few things that need attention after that contract is signed.

It's easy to get lost in the excitement of your first or second client. People are paying you money to do what you love, you're in the zone, and you're super excited to dive into the project and prove your worth. Absolutely, do your thing, but remember that you have life responsibilities outside of the project. This includes tending to your mental and physical health. Take breaks; get that exercise in; stock up on drinks and healthy snacks; and socialize a bit, even if it just means asking your grocery store cashier how his day is going. Your body and mind will thank you as the weeks go on!

All the major components of this project are detailed in your contract, but there are a few highly technical things that you need to take care of on your end to ensure a smooth build. In this chapter we'll cover the three main processes when it's time to start working: architecting, building, and deploying.

Architecting

Architecting a site essentially means that you're planning and designing the build: What languages and tools will you use? How will the business logic be implemented? What color scheme will you incorporate and what will the layout be? What happens when a user clicks that button over there?

In other words, architecting is the design of the technical, functional, and visual components of a website before its development and deployment.

Programs like Balsamiq, Adobe XD, and Sketch allow you to create wireframes, mockups and prototypes to help visualize the frontend of your site or application in various fidelities. Additionally, Photoshop enables you slice up your images so you can convert it to HTML & CSS. XD and Sketch are both free to use, while Balsamiq and Photoshop are subscription-based.

Conversely, you can go old-school and use pen and paper to sketch out your designs, or even use CSS and HTML to go direct to prototyping if you have a strong vision. It really just depends on your level of comfort with design tools and what feels best for you.

A rundown of common architecting terms and techniques:

Wireframe: low-fidelity, minimalistic blueprints used as placeholders to represent a design or idea.

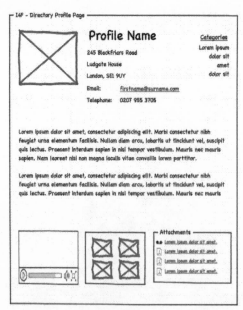

A wireframe created with Balsamiq

Mockup: a static, high-profile visual design draft, used to represent the structure of information, visualize the content, and demonstrate the basic functionalities. Mockups provide visual details like typography and colors.

Seen with gridlines inside Photoshop, this is an example of a mockup webpage that contains the structure of information, visualization of content, and basic site functionality.

Prototype: Closest to the real thing as possible, a prototype mimics the look, structure, and functionality of the site or app.

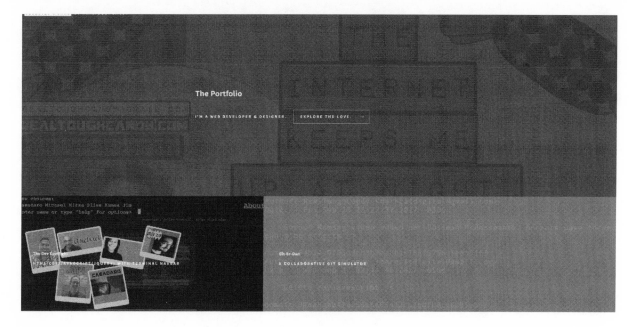

Prototype of portfolio landing page

Depending on the client, your proposal and contract, and your business plan, you might provide some of these items for your client to look over prior to building the site. It isn't the best feeling having your earliest work picked apart, but it's **much** easier to make changes early on rather than during the build. Additionally, wireframes, mockups, and prototypes all build trust with your client by showing that you have a disciplined, multi-stage process. Embrace these changes the client requests while they're easy tweaks! This interaction also validates the client when they see some of their ideas in action.

My workflow: For fullstack development, I tend to experiment with HTML and CSS for the frontend right away, sketch the backend with pen and paper (largely consisting of boxes and lines with pseudocode where applicable), then use Sketch or XD to transform the HTML/CSS design into a mockup with build notes and additional photos and illustrations of buttons, forms, and other site components. I'll also have a code editor open throughout the process to jot down additional ideas for the build. Sometimes I'll use UML if there's significant OOP involved. I rarely build prototypes unless a client requests it and agrees to pay for them in writing. My mockups are generally high-fidelity and work fine for guiding my front-end builds.

Building

You're a web developer, so you naturally take the reins as soon as your vision is solidified. It's coding time.

Be very aware of your time management and life responsibilities outside your web development work. **Time runs out *fast*.** It sounds obvious, but planning your workweek can really help organize your life and keep your projects manageable. I'm a natural procrastinator, but waiting two days before deadline to create a client website was one of the worst decisions I've ever made as a professional.

Time mismanagement can work for writing college papers, but not for freelancing. The anxiety of missing a deadline with your reputation and paycheck on the line just isn't worth it.

One time-management technique used in tech is the Pomodoro technique. Basically, it's an interval system that rewards you with a nice little break for every 25 minutes you stay focused on your work. There are also Pomodoro timer apps for your smartphone. Many people swear by this technique. To be totally honest, both my focus and brain are too chaotic for this structured technique, but it might work really well for you.

Build Checklist

✓ Project has been architected/wireframed/mocked/prototyped.

✓ File structure is clean and logical (even if it's solely your build).

✓ Project has a backup location and is regularly updated with the latest copy.

✓ Project has hosting and domain name secured.

✓ Project follows best security practices, including HTTPS encryption, robust
passwords, appropriate privilege levels for users and admins, etc.

✓ Code is commented appropriately (even if it's solely your build).

✓ Code follows best practices and has been refactored.

✓ Client is receiving regular status updates via email.

✓ Client receives prompt, helpful answers when s/he asks questions.

Deployment (Hosting)

Somewhere along the line, web hosting and other webmaster tasks were relegated to the daily duties of web developers. Make no mistake, configuring a server or even just getting your account set up for maximum efficiency can be a real challenge. It's also a departure from what you're probably used to doing on a regular basis with your personal projects, since clients also often need email servers configured along with other additional server-based services, such as cron jobs. Let's talk about a few hosting configurations to get you prepared. We'll go over traditional web hosting along with cloud hosting and some use cases for each.

Traditional Web Hosting: This is a workhorse. You finish your website, fire up FileZilla with that sweet (S)FTP action, and get to transferring your site the server. A couple minutes later, and you're live on the web. It's been done like this for decades, and it's not going out of style anytime soon. If you haven't explored web hosting yet, check out the various service providers and see who can fulfill your business requirements the best. My personal choice is Namecheap. The name sounds tacky, but their first-year prices are insanely affordable, and their follow-up prices aren't too shabby, either. In addition, their customer support is outstanding. I've been on chat with them dozens of times during my freelance career and I've had nothing but fast and effective service, whether it's solving an email server issue or resetting my password after I guessed it wrong for the 20th time.

Traditional web hosting comes in two main flavors: shared and VPS.

Shared hosting: this is when you share a little space on a server with other customers who want to save money. There's nothing intrinsically wrong with this setup, but think of it as living in an apartment in a not-so-nice part of town. Sure, you have your own space and locks on the door, but the walls are thin, people are on edge, and you never know when a party is going to infiltrate the adjacent unit, keeping you awake until your alarm goes off at 8 AM.

Also, why the heck is there a person outside your door with a lampshade on his head stumbling around? Shared hosting is good for low-scale personal projects, but for most client work, you'll want to upgrade to either VPS or the cloud. It's not the fact that you're a bad housekeeper on shared hosting; it's the fact that other people on your same partition are hogging resources, threatening security, and slowing down your own operation at odd hours.

Don't send your client to a bad part of virtual town where doors get kicked down. Note also that shared hosting doesn't give you root access, which can really put a damper on your project and its deployment.

 Shared hosting pairs nicely with: Personal projects, demos.

VPS Hosting: A step up is VPS hosting, or virtual private server. Whereas shared hosting is like an apartment unit, VPS is like a townhouse. You have neighbors, but you have your own walls and your own stairwells: security is tighter and privacy is greater. VPS is slightly more expensive than shared web hosting but the upgrade is almost always worth it.

 VPS pairs nicely with: WordPress, smaller client sites.

Cloud Hosting: The cloud is fast, flexible, and uses the power of multiple servers to host your site or application. VPS and cloud hosting have a lot in common, but cloud hosting has a major benefit in that you only pay for the resources you use, rather than a flat fee. Additionally, cloud hosting is designed to scale so that you don't have to worry about your server crashing if your client suddenly receives a burst of traffic from a pay-per-click marketing campaign, wild Black Friday sale, or maybe some interactive app that expects bursts of visitors at exact times of the day.

You've probably heard of AWS, Google Cloud, and Heroku. These are just a few examples of cloud platforms. Learning even the basic ways of the cloud can be a challenge, especially if you're not familiar with command line operations. But with some reading up of the documentation (and perhaps even a Udemy course), you'll be able to take control of the cloud space. If you don't want to mess with the nitty gritty, there are also managed cloud hosting providers like Cloudways and Rackspace that take care of many of the pain points associated with cloud deployment and maintenance.

There are many nuanced differences between each cloud provider. You could start off with experimenting using Heroku, which offers a free tier for small personal projects.

 The cloud pairs nicely with: High-traffic sites, clients who want the best, apps with various backends and databases (Node, Go, Python, MongoDB, etc.).

	VPS Hosting	Cloud Hosting
Server Deployment and Management	Yes	Yes
Server Sharing Model	Private Server	Dedicated Cloud Server
Scalability (auto/manual)	Yes	Yes
Low Cost	Yes	Yes
Pay As You Go	No	Yes
Flexibility	No	Yes
Customization	Yes	Yes
Security	Yes	Yes
Instant Provisioning	No	Yes (in managed hosting)
Performance	Depends on vendor	Fast
Reliability	Yes	Yes
Multiple Data Centers	Depends on vendor	Yes

VPS and cloud hosting have numerous similarities, but the cloud offers additional dynamic features like faster performance and a pay-as-you-go model.

Deployment Times

Things will go wrong when you're ready to deploy. A *lot* of things. From forgotten MySQL credentials to missing files, the best way to prepare for this event is to give yourself a wide berth and plenty of time to fail and recover.

For example, when I'm deploying on a host that's new to my web development arsenal, I give myself at *least* an entire workday (i.e. seven to eight hours) to explore the interface, read the docs, upload a dummy project, identify common failures and fix them, along with stage the final production build so that I can go live as soon as my client gives the final approval. There was one time when Namecheap customer support had to unlock my account *twenty times* in one day (don't ask). Thankfully, I had given myself ample time to deal with that sort of thing.

Final Meeting

No matter how long it takes to deploy, be sure to provide your client with the appropriate documentation, login credentials, and other key items they need to use their site. This can be done in a variety of ways but I like to have a final meeting with the client, show off the new site, answer questions, do some basic training, and officially wrap up the project.

What you provide your client also depends on the level of management you'll be doing for them – if you'll be the one writing blog posts for them, for example, there's no need to provide them with publishing permissions.

Chapter Summary

In this chapter, we covered the heavy lifting of your freelance operation, including planning your project, building the project, time management, and deploying. You have many options for architecting, whether good ol' fashioned pen and paper or something more advanced like CSS right in the browser. Hosting options are varied, and all depend on what kind of project you're working on. In the next chapter, we'll wrap it up and talk about taking the steps to take your business to the next level.

Chapter 13

Post-Noob

In this chapter we're going to discuss some techniques you can use to level up your business.

"Aftercare"

In the medical profession, patients are often given a set of instructions to follow once they get home. They are given a phone number to call in case they have questions, and many times have a date set for a follow-up appointment. This aftercare ensures they are able to reach their goal of healing without constant professional supervision.

Similarly, your freelance clients should have an aftercare routine. But, instead of helping them heal from back surgery, *this* routine helps them feel validated about their decision to hire you, educated about their new tech product, and connected to you and your business after they make that final payment. There are many ways to set up this routine, but one thing that can work well is an exit packet.

Exit packets are emailed to clients a few days after you get the final approval and payment for their project. They include various materials that emphasize that you care about them and value their business—all while wanting to improve your services. For example, you could include a summary of the work produced (in a casual tone rather than legal language), documentation for how to operate "user serviceable" parts of their website such as blog areas, your contact information if something catastrophic happens, all third-party contact information for their web host, along with a brief survey to collect their feedback. While you may not like everything people write (or type) about your business, use those critiques to motivate you to improve those areas. You should also use the good reviews as social proof and put them in you feedback database for later use on your website and promotional materials.

Want to Earn More? Never Stop Learning & Implementing

It's tough to set aside dedicated learning time while working full-time and tending to your personal life, but always be thinking about what you can learn next to offer as a service. For example, learning PHP opened a huge door for me, since that allowed me to customize WordPress backends in addition to troubleshoot them. Keep up with the trends, explore new languages, frameworks, and tools (or expand your knowledge of your current collection), pick out what you think you can monetize, and go for it.

Integration

Another good money-maker involves integration. This one took a while for me to recognize, and it was only after I entered my first enterprise job where I saw its power.

I worked at a data company where I built and maintained large ecommerce applications for enterprise clients. These apps weren't your typical WooCommerce or even Shopify customers; these were companies with hundreds of thousands of SKUs, multiple physical locations, in-house shipping departments – all which used instances of our company's proprietary software and aging (yet highly capable) IBM AS/400 server. I learned a *lot* about business, process-oriented thinking, and how much measurable financial value software developers create, especially in the long term. I mean, a single developer can create **millions** of dollars in profits for a company over a five or ten year period. Think about that for a minute!

Aside from monthly maintenance and hosting charges, the company earned a large chunk of its revenue from integration tools. Consider: When a fish lure sells at Physical Location A, and then a fish lure sells online, how is that updated to reflect real-time inventory? Certainly employees can't be expected to login and subtract an item each time it sells at the physical location. Or what if a high-volume client is in the bike rental business? Certainly employees can't be expected to run back to a computer terminal every time a walk-in customer checks out the last bike, hoping to update inventory before an online customer snatches a non-existent rental. Conversely, if an online customer reserves a bike, how will the employee know to set it aside, away from view of the walk-in customers? Definitely not refreshing a webpage all day to check statuses.

From shipping, to pricing and invoicing, to customer relationships, and whatever else, think about integration with other aspects of your clients' business. Owning a business means owning problems, managing a business means managing problems, and working at a business means working with problems. You have the ability to solve all of these multi-level problems with your skills. And *that* is what really adds value to a business and allows you to charge handsomely.

Collaboration & Volunteering

I have a lot of interests outside developing software. Music, local food, performance art, old-school gaming, kombucha, nature and wildlife, betta fish, driving around checking out Christmas lights...The list goes on. The thing is, all of these areas rely on software, from music production to scanning inventory of platinum dumbo-ear halfmoon bettas.

I strike up conversations with approachable people whenever I can who are outside my industry. Many times it's just a chit-chat, but other times it leads to business opportunities. Specifically, opportunities that emerge through collaboration and volunteering.

Collaboration and volunteering not only get your name out there, but they also send a message that you're an active, community-minded individual who likes to work with others. This is great for lead-generation! Collaboration and volunteering are also *amazing* for social media exposure – again, another avenue for generating leads. Let's go over a few examples of how you can leverage your collaboration and volunteering activities to generate interest in your freelance business.

Example 1. Say you enjoy fine art. A local artist you met a few months ago at a gallery opening debuted his piece, which explored the intersection of technology and society in the 21st century. You enjoy this guy's work and had a chance to talk during the gallery opening. Why not send him an email asking if he'd be interested in collaborating – creating a new piece that involved a software component or website developed by you? Think about how much buzz this would create on social media as well as in his own social circle, in addition to any external media coverage. It could open up a huge avenue for leads while expanding your skillset in the process.

Example 2. Say you love local outdoor music festivals. These fests are **always** looking for volunteers. So, you decide to volunteer as a ticket-taker...But don't just leave it at that! After your shift when it's party time, put on a piece of clothing advertising your business, take selfies with some of the band members who stuck around to hang out for the after-party (tagging them using your business accounts), hand out business cards to those you're socializing with, do some guerrilla marketing...You get the idea.

After the party, it's the after-party...And then time to secure a freelance client or two.

Example 3. You can also go the traditional route and volunteer to help build a website for a non-profit you believe in. You're not only helping your community, but getting your name out there to everybody involved in the non-profit. And when that place ends up getting media exposure, you're even luckier with more free advertising.

Remember, nearly every human activity these days relies on software, so don't ever think that one of your interests is too unrelated to what you do.

Chapter 14

Conclusion

In this book, you learned how to get started as a newcomer to the freelance web development world. Hopefully you gained some valuable insight along with inspiration to start taking those first steps in establishing yourself as a capable, motivated freelancer.

Freelancing has so many benefits, but not every day is going to be a winner. There are cranky clients, sites that break, and some days you just may not be in the mood to code and create. That's OK! The important part is to just stick with it. There is so much room for you in this field and if you want to succeed, you *can* and you *will.*

I did my best to include all the techniques, methods, tips, tricks, and actionable steps needed to be an excellent freelance newbie, but you'll probably come across situations outside the scope of this book.

If you have any questions or would like feedback on your own freelance website or business plan, feel free to join the RealToughCandy Discord server.

Direct link: https://discord.gg/88Q4v3m

Post your question in the #general text channel and be sure to tag me. (I try to log on daily but sometimes miss posts unless I'm tagged). It's a fun, welcoming, respectful, and motivating community with a diverse array of developers. You're also welcome to join even if you don't need additional freelance help.

Good luck in your new freelance career! I'm rooting for you!

Appendix A: Do I Need To Know WordPress?

Over one-third of the web uses WordPress. From that statistic alone, It's no wonder why so many creative agencies and freelancers offer it as their flagship service. In addition, WordPress is:

- Easy to deploy and maintain
- Plugin-based: you don't have to be a PHP whiz to integrate great features
- End-user friendly
- Open-source (free as in beer, free as in freedom)
- Highly scalable

WordPress: User-Serviceable, Human-Readable

All of these benefits are nice, but does that mean you have to offer it? The short answer is no. However, it's an excellent money maker. If you're already familiar with WordPress, absolutely consider integrating it into your business plan. If you're not familiar with WordPress, I would suggest you at least become familiar with its basic usage. Work on setting up a local copy, experiment with features and plugins, and get familiar with the file structure. While WordPress is powered by PHP and MySQL on the backend, you don't need to know PHP or SQL in order to create websites for clients. If you need to customize it and you can't find a suitable plugin, you can always outsource the task if it's beyond your current skill level.

As you find more clients, listen to their needs, and strategize on solving their business problems, you will find that WordPress is often an ideal fit.

The *other* reason I'm so enthusiastic about using WordPress is because of its straightforward admin panel. This means you can confidently set up a user account for your client and they can take care of the rest, whether it's updating plugins (one click), publishing a blog post, adding users, or whatever other common task that would be more of a time-sink than a money-maker if they had me do it.

This was true even as a total newbie: the ten minutes of billable time (or even a flat fee) for whatever menial task just wasn't worth it to me. You also run the risk of clients calling you up every hour with another small issue, many of which will have you wondering if it's even worth the hassle of sending an invoice. It's much more efficient to give them a tour of the user-serviceable parts, direct them to human-readable documentation for common and simple tasks, and give them the freedom to do it on their own time.

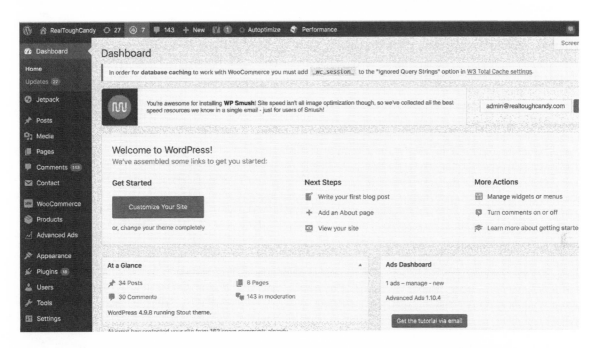

Above: the admin panel of WordPress is easy to use for non-technical end users.

> WordPress or not, always maintain your own copy of any site you build for a client. You never know what they'll do to change the look and functionality of your site once they have access to the code. Many times it's for the worse and you won't be able to exhibit this site in your portfolio or other promotional materials.

Bottom line, explore WordPress as a solution for your clients. Even if you've never used it, you'll be able to pick up the basics just fine. If you do decide to go full WordPress mode, you can either learn PHP and MySQL or hire somebody else to make plugins. I was building sites for profit before I even knew how to code, and it turned into a consistently ideal solution for my clients.

Appendix B: Common Client Objections

Clients are going to ask you lots of questions – that's a good thing! However, some of these questions can be a bit tricky to answer. Other times they are the product of passive-aggressive behavior and it's challenging to pivot the conversation to a more proactive dialogue. Yet other times, they have genuine and legitimate objections that need to be addressed head-on. Let's go through a few of these client objections and discuss some ways you might respond to them.

My son said he could make me a site for free.

I've had people say this to me so many times and you have to wonder: Why call if you have somebody who can do it for free? Are you trying to get me to do it for free or are you just calling to make the announcement? People have mentioned this to me so much that I'm mostly beyond a blood pressure spike when it's asked. Instead, I'm equipped to answer their question in a bullet-point fashion. People love bullet-points. I also remain positive and conversational because while people love bullet-points, they *don't* love smart-alecks.

"Your son sounds technically inclined, and that's great! But here's the thing...Lots of people can code, most people can use the drag-and-drop sites, no doubt. But I'm a little different. I'm a professional web developer with a history of successful sites and my speciality is:

- results-driven web development,
- architecting your features to reflect your business needs,
- building something that's scalable so your site can easily grow with your business,
- optimizing your SEO so people can find your site,
- ensuring your site is safe and secure from hackers,
- testing your site so that it works on all browsers and devices,
- having regular backups of everything in case something catastrophic happens,
- and really putting that professional touch on your site so people take your business seriously."

And then I go on: "I mean, really, it's not just about the code – they've actually taught monkeys to code. So you know, you're totally welcome to go with what your son can offer. I'm sure he could make a great looking web page, absolutely. But what I offer is a results-driven web presence using a very technical and proven process [explain process], I make my clients lots of money, I send them a lot – a **lot** of visitors – and I definitely urge you to check out my portfolio to see what other businesses have been saying about me. And definitely read their case studies and check out their sites I built with my process. People keep coming to me because I understand their business needs and my team and I transform those needs into a very successful digital arm of their business."

I don't like to play cat and mouse with objection scenarios like this – I get right to the point of what I do, and differentiate myself from the crowd of sons, aunts, and pet ferrets that can make their site for free. It really helps when you explain that you have a process, along with reciting the phases of that process. Like I explained in the business plan chapter – the *processes,* and the professional organization of those processes, are where the value and money is.

Can I get that family discount or what?

If a potential client is a referral from a family or friend, you'll probably get asked about a family or friend discount. Unless this person is a starter client, be assertive with your pricing. Lowering your pricing because of a deal-seeker is the first step in lowering your worth as a freelancer – financially, socially, and psychologically. Remember, you're here to make a living, not participate in Oprah-style giveaways or agree to garage sale prices. When somebody outside my starter client roster asks for a discount or otherwise implies they don't want to pay my asking price, I very simply say, "I do give a 10% military discount and I'd be happy to apply that to any project if you qualify. Other than that, my prices are industry standard for the area. Any lower and I would have to cut some features on your project, and I definitely don't want to be doing that."

If they keep pushing for a lower price after that, that's a client from hell alert. Refer them to Upwork and look for higher-quality clients.

Can you create X, Y, and Z features while you're at it? Those sound pretty straightforward and it would make the site so much better. You'd really be helping me out.

Techies have worked hard over the generations to abstract the inner workings of software for end users. It's no coincidence clients usually don't see how technically intense our job is: it was engineered that way! What may seem like an easy add-on from a user standpoint can end up being a weeks-long feature request. When your client requests a "simple" request that really isn't, explain to your customer that a lot of work is necessary to make these pieces of the machine work. This is the one area where you *should* explain your process in detail (including architecting, testing, and everything in between). Namedrop tools, languages, and technologies if need be.

Most often, after giving them a little tour under the hood of the web, your client will have a new appreciation for the web development process. From there, you can give them a quote for the feature.

However, should they still insist it's simple after you've explained everything clearly and professionally, this is a warning sign you're dealing with a client from hell who doesn't respect your craft. Give them a price quote for the feature, and if they grumble about it, fulfill your contract as you normally would, get paid, and don't take any more work from them. Bad clients are just not worth it.

52478400R00062

Made in the USA
Columbia, SC
03 March 2019